Dynamic Leadership

Essential Qualities and Habits of Successful Leaders

Dexter Allen

The presentation of the information is without contract or any type of guarantee assurance. The trademarks that are used are without any consent, and the publication of the trademark is without permission or backing by the trademark owner. All trademarks and brands within this book are for clarifying purposes only and are the owned by the owners themselves, not affiliated with this document.

Table of Contents

Chapter 1

Introduction

The Importance of Dynamic Leadership

Dynamic leadership is a crucial element in the modern organizational landscape, where change is the only constant. Leaders who can adapt, innovate, and inspire are essential for navigating the complexities of today's business environment. Dynamic leadership is not just about reacting to change but proactively driving it. It involves a blend of vision, flexibility, resilience, and emotional intelligence to lead teams through uncertainty and toward success.

The significance of dynamic leadership is multifaceted. At its core, it enables organizations to remain competitive and relevant. In an era defined by rapid technological advancements and shifting market demands, businesses must be agile. Dynamic leaders possess the foresight to anticipate changes and the agility to pivot strategies accordingly. This ability to adapt ensures that organizations can seize new opportunities and mitigate potential threats.

Consider the case of Netflix, which transitioned from a DVD rental service to a leading streaming platform. This strategic shift was driven by dynamic leadership that recognized the impending decline of physical media and the rise of digital content consumption. By embracing change and innovating continuously, Netflix maintained its market position and set a new industry standard. This example underscores how dynamic leadership can transform potential disruptions into avenues for growth.

Dynamic leadership also fosters a culture of continuous improvement and learning within organizations. Leaders who embody this style encourage their teams to embrace experimentation and view failures as learning opportunities. This mindset cultivates an environment where creativity and innovation can flourish. When employees feel empowered to take risks and challenge the status quo, they are more likely to develop groundbreaking solutions that drive the organization forward.

Emotional intelligence plays a pivotal role in dynamic leadership. Effective leaders understand and manage their own emotions while being attuned to the emotions of others. This emotional awareness enables them to build strong relationships, foster trust, and create a positive work environment. For instance, during times of organizational change, employees may experience anxiety and resistance. A dynamic leader with high emotional intelligence can address these concerns empathetically, easing the transition and maintaining team morale.

Communication is another critical aspect of dynamic leadership. Leaders must articulate their vision clearly and inspire others to buy into that vision. Transparent and effective communication ensures that everyone in the organization understands the goals, the reasons behind strategic shifts, and their role in achieving success. This alignment is crucial for maintaining focus and cohesion, especially during periods of change.

Consider the leadership of Satya Nadella at Microsoft. When he took over as CEO, he communicated a clear vision of transforming Microsoft into a cloud-first, mobile-first company. His transparent communication and emphasis on a growth mindset revitalized the company's culture and spurred innovation. Under his leadership, Microsoft regained its position as a technology leader, demonstrating the power of dynamic leadership in driving organizational success.

Dynamic leadership also involves making tough decisions swiftly and confidently. In a rapidly changing environment, hesitation can lead to missed opportunities or exacerbated challenges. Leaders must be decisive, weighing the available information and potential outcomes to make informed choices. This decisiveness instills confidence in the team and provides a clear direction, even amidst uncertainty.

Moreover, dynamic leaders are adept at building and leading diverse teams. Diversity brings a multitude of perspectives and ideas, which are invaluable for innovation and problem-solving. Leaders who value diversity and inclusion create an environment where all voices are heard and respected. This inclusivity not only enhances team performance but also reflects positively on the organization's culture and reputation.

In addition to fostering diversity, dynamic leaders prioritize the development of their team members. They invest in training, mentorship, and professional growth opportunities. By nurturing talent and providing avenues for advancement, leaders ensure that their teams are equipped to handle future challenges. This commitment to development also enhances employee engagement and retention, as individuals feel valued and supported in their career journeys.

Adaptability is a hallmark of dynamic leadership. The ability to pivot strategies and approaches in response to evolving circumstances is essential. This adaptability is not confined to external changes but also involves internal adjustments. Leaders must be willing to reassess their own assumptions, seek feedback, and continuously refine their leadership style. This commitment to self-improvement ensures that they remain effective and relevant in their roles.

Furthermore, dynamic leadership extends beyond organizational boundaries. Leaders must navigate complex stakeholder relationships, including customers, partners, and the broader community. Building and maintaining these relationships requires a nuanced understanding of diverse interests and the ability to find common ground. Effective leaders engage with stakeholders proactively, fostering collaboration and building trust.

The impact of dynamic leadership on organizational performance cannot be overstated. Research consistently shows that companies with dynamic leaders outperform their peers. These organizations are more innovative, resilient, and capable of sustaining long-term growth. The influence of dynamic leadership extends to employee satisfaction and engagement as well. When leaders inspire and empower their teams, employees are more motivated and committed to achieving organizational goals.

Dynamic leadership is also critical in times of crisis. The COVID-19 pandemic, for instance, tested the resilience and adaptability of leaders worldwide. Those who successfully navigated the crisis demonstrated agility, empathy, and strategic foresight. They were able to pivot operations, support their teams, and find new ways to serve their customers. This crisis highlighted the essential qualities of dynamic leadership and underscored its importance in ensuring organizational survival and recovery.

Purpose and Scope of the Book

Leadership is a journey, often fraught with challenges and opportunities alike. This book aims to serve as a compass for those navigating the complexities of contemporary leadership. Its purpose is twofold: to illuminate the essential qualities and habits that define successful leaders and to provide practical, actionable insights for developing these traits. Whether you are an emerging leader seeking to build your foundation or an experienced one looking to refine your skills, this book offers a comprehensive guide to dynamic leadership.

Understanding the scope of this book is crucial for maximizing its benefits. It is structured to cover a wide array of topics, each critical to the development of effective leadership. From self-awareness and emotional intelligence to communication and innovation, the chapters are designed to build upon one another, creating a cohesive and holistic approach to leadership. This structure ensures that readers can progress systematically, gaining a deeper understanding of each aspect of leadership before moving on to the next.

The journey begins with an exploration of dynamic leadership, setting the stage for the subsequent chapters. Here, you will delve into the definition and evolution of leadership theories, understanding how they have shaped contemporary practices. This foundation is critical, as it provides the context needed to appreciate the nuances of dynamic leadership. By examining case studies of successful leaders, you will gain insights into how these principles are applied in real-world scenarios.

Self-awareness is the cornerstone of effective leadership. It involves a deep understanding of one's strengths, weaknesses, and the impact of one's behavior on others. This book emphasizes the importance of self-assessment tools and techniques to help leaders identify areas for improvement. By fostering a culture of continuous self-improvement, leaders can remain adaptable and resilient in the face of change. Emotional intelligence, a key component of self-awareness, will be explored in depth, providing strategies for managing emotions and building strong relationships.

Communication is another critical area covered in this book. Effective communication is not just about conveying information but also about listening and understanding. Leaders must be adept at both verbal and non-verbal communication, ensuring that their message is clear and impactful. This book offers practical advice on how to provide constructive feedback, communicate vision and goals, and foster an environment of open dialogue. By mastering these skills, leaders can inspire and motivate their teams, driving them toward shared objectives.

The book also addresses the significance of emotional intelligence in leadership. Understanding and managing one's emotions, as well as empathizing with others, is crucial for building trust and rapport. This section delves into the four components of emotional intelligence: self-awareness, self-regulation, social awareness, and relationship management. By developing these skills, leaders can navigate interpersonal dynamics more effectively, leading to stronger, more cohesive teams.

Innovation and creativity are indispensable in today's fast-paced world. This book explores techniques for fostering a culture of innovation, encouraging leaders to think outside the box and embrace new ideas. Real-world examples of innovative leadership provide inspiration and practical insights into overcoming barriers to creativity. Leaders will learn how to create an environment where innovation can thrive, driving their organizations toward sustained success.

The book's practical approach ensures that readers can apply the concepts and strategies discussed in their own leadership journeys. Each chapter includes actionable advice, real-world examples, and reflective exercises designed to reinforce learning. By engaging with these materials, readers can develop a personalized leadership plan that aligns with their unique strengths and goals.

In addition to individual development, this book emphasizes the importance of building and leading effective teams. Leaders must be able to identify and nurture talent, creating an environment where team members can excel. This involves understanding team dynamics, fostering collaboration, and managing conflicts constructively. The book provides strategies for building high-performing teams, ensuring that leaders can harness the collective strengths of their members.

Furthermore, the book addresses the challenges and opportunities presented by diversity and inclusion. In today's globalized world, leaders must be adept at navigating diverse cultures and perspectives. This book offers insights into how to create an inclusive environment where all team members feel valued and respected. By embracing diversity, leaders can drive innovation, improve decision-making, and enhance organizational performance.

The book also explores the role of ethics and integrity in leadership. Leaders are often faced with difficult decisions that test their moral compass. This book provides guidance on how to navigate ethical dilemmas, ensuring that leaders act with integrity and uphold their values. By fostering a culture of ethical behavior, leaders can build trust and credibility, both within their organizations and with external stakeholders.

Ultimately, the purpose of this book is to equip leaders with the knowledge and tools they need to succeed in today's dynamic environment. By exploring a broad range of topics, from self-awareness and communication to innovation and ethics, this book offers a comprehensive guide to effective leadership. It is designed to be both informative and practical, providing actionable insights that leaders can apply in their own contexts.

The scope of this book ensures that it is relevant to leaders at all stages of their careers. Whether you are just starting out or looking to refine your skills, the concepts and strategies discussed in this book will provide valuable guidance. By engaging with the materials and reflecting on your own experiences, you can develop a personalized leadership plan that aligns with your unique strengths and goals.

How to Use This Book

Embarking on a journey to understand and master dynamic leadership requires a structured and strategic approach. This book is designed as a comprehensive guide to help you navigate the multifaceted aspects of leadership, providing you with both theoretical insights and practical tools. To maximize the benefits of this book, it's important to understand how to use its contents effectively. Here's a roadmap to get the most out of your reading experience.

Firstly, approach this book with an open mind and a willingness to reflect on your leadership style. Each chapter is crafted to build upon the previous one, creating a cohesive narrative that enhances your understanding of dynamic leadership. Start by reading the introductory chapters to familiarize yourself with the foundational concepts. These chapters lay the groundwork by defining dynamic leadership, exploring its evolution, and highlighting its relevance in today's fast-paced world.

As you move through the book, take the time to engage with the self-assessment tools and reflective exercises provided. These activities are designed to help you gain a deeper understanding of your strengths and areas for improvement. For instance, when reading about self-awareness, utilize the provided self-assessment questionnaires to evaluate your emotional intelligence and leadership style. Reflect on the results and consider how they align with your experiences and goals. This introspective approach will enable you to personalize the insights and strategies discussed, making them more applicable to your unique context.

One of the key features of this book is its practical focus. Each chapter includes actionable advice and real-world examples that illustrate how the concepts can be applied in various leadership scenarios. When reading about communication, for example, you'll find tips on how to craft clear and compelling messages, listen actively, and provide constructive feedback. These practical insights are meant to be implemented, so don't just read passively. Take notes, highlight key points, and think about how you can incorporate these strategies into your daily interactions with your team.

In addition to practical tips, the book offers numerous case studies of successful leaders from different industries. These case studies provide valuable lessons and inspiration, showing how dynamic leadership principles have been effectively applied in real-world situations. Pay close attention to these examples and consider how the strategies used by these leaders can be adapted to your own context. For instance, if a case study highlights how a leader successfully navigated a major organizational change, think about how you can apply similar approaches in your own change management efforts.

Another important aspect of using this book effectively is to engage with the reflective exercises at the end of each chapter. These exercises are designed to reinforce the concepts discussed and encourage you to think critically about your leadership journey. For example, after reading about fostering a culture of innovation, you might be prompted to reflect on how you currently encourage creativity within your team and identify specific actions you can take to enhance this culture. By actively engaging with these exercises, you'll deepen your understanding and be better prepared to apply the lessons learned.

While the book is designed to be read sequentially, it is also structured in a way that allows you to jump to specific chapters that are most relevant to your current needs. If you're facing a particular leadership challenge, such as managing a diverse team or navigating a crisis, feel free to skip ahead to the chapters that address these topics. Each chapter is self-contained and provides comprehensive insights and strategies, ensuring that you can gain valuable knowledge even if you don't read the book cover to cover in one go.

Additionally, this book encourages you to seek feedback and engage in discussions with others as you progress through the chapters. Leadership is not a solitary endeavor; it involves interacting with and influencing others. Share the insights and strategies you gain from this book with your colleagues, mentors, and team members. Engage in discussions about how these concepts can be applied in your organization and seek feedback on your leadership approach. This collaborative learning process will enrich your understanding and help you refine your leadership skills.

To further enhance your learning experience, consider keeping a leadership journal as you read through the book. Use this journal to document your reflections, insights, and action plans. Write down specific goals you want to achieve and track your progress over time. For example, if you set a goal to improve your communication skills, use your journal to record instances where you applied the strategies discussed in the book and reflect on the outcomes. This practice of journaling will not only reinforce your learning but also serve as a valuable resource for future reference.

Remember that leadership development is an ongoing journey. The insights and strategies you gain from this book are meant to be revisited and refined over time. As you apply the concepts in your leadership practice, take note of what works well and what needs adjustment. Reflect on your experiences, seek feedback, and continue to learn and grow. This iterative process of learning and improvement is at the heart of dynamic leadership.

Finally, use this book as a source of inspiration and motivation. Leadership can be challenging, and there will be times when you face setbacks and obstacles. During these times, revisit the stories of successful leaders and remind yourself of the impact that effective leadership can have. Reflect on your own progress and the positive changes you've made. Let this book serve as a reminder of your commitment to becoming a dynamic leader capable of driving positive change in your organization and beyond.

Overview of Key Themes

Understanding the core themes of dynamic leadership is essential for anyone aspiring to lead effectively in today's complex and fast-paced world. This chapter provides an overview of the key themes that form the foundation of dynamic leadership. These themes are interconnected, each contributing to a holistic approach that empowers leaders to navigate challenges, inspire their teams, and drive meaningful change.

One of the central themes of dynamic leadership is self-awareness. At its core, self-awareness involves a deep understanding of one's own strengths, weaknesses, values, and impact on others. Leaders who are self-aware are better equipped to make informed decisions, manage their emotions, and build authentic relationships. Consider a leader who consistently reflects on their interactions and seeks feedback from peers and subordinates. This leader is likely to be more attuned to their blind spots and more open to personal growth. Self-awareness is not a static trait but a continuous process of reflection and adjustment.

Closely related to self-awareness is emotional intelligence, another critical theme. Emotional intelligence encompasses the ability to recognize, understand, and manage one's own emotions, as well as the emotions of others. Leaders with high emotional intelligence can navigate complex interpersonal dynamics, build trust, and foster a positive work environment. For example, a leader who can remain calm and composed under pressure sets a tone of stability and confidence for their team. Moreover, by demonstrating empathy and active listening, they can create a culture of openness and mutual respect.

Communication is an indispensable theme in dynamic leadership. Effective leaders must be able to convey their vision, goals, and expectations clearly and persuasively. This involves not just speaking and writing, but also listening actively and providing constructive feedback. Imagine a leader who holds regular team meetings to discuss progress, address concerns, and celebrate successes. This leader is practicing transparent communication, which helps to build trust and alignment within the team. Additionally, adapting communication styles to suit different audiences and contexts is a crucial skill for any leader.

Visionary thinking is another vital theme. Leaders must be able to see beyond the immediate challenges and envision the future direction of their organization. This ability to articulate a compelling vision inspires and motivates others to work towards a common goal. Take, for instance, a leader who envisions a more sustainable and innovative organization. By clearly communicating this vision and aligning it with the company's values and strategic goals, they can galvanize their team to strive for continuous improvement and creativity.

Innovation and creativity are essential themes in dynamic leadership, particularly in today's rapidly changing world. Effective leaders encourage a culture of experimentation and risk-taking, where new ideas are welcomed and valued. Consider a leader who implements regular brainstorming sessions and innovation challenges to stimulate creative thinking within their team. Such practices not only generate new ideas but also empower team members to take ownership of their contributions. By fostering an environment where innovation can thrive, leaders can drive their organization towards sustained success.

Adaptability is another key theme. The ability to remain flexible and open to change is crucial in a world where the only constant is change itself. Leaders who can adapt their strategies and approaches in response to evolving circumstances are better positioned to navigate uncertainties and seize new opportunities. Picture a leader who quickly adjusts their team's priorities in response to a sudden market shift. This leader's adaptability ensures that the team remains focused and resilient in the face of unexpected challenges.

Ethics and integrity are foundational themes in dynamic leadership. Leaders are often faced with difficult decisions that test their moral compass. Upholding ethical standards and acting with integrity are crucial for building trust and credibility. Imagine a leader who consistently makes decisions that align with their values and the values of their organization, even when faced with pressure to compromise. This leader sets a powerful example for their team and reinforces a culture of ethical behavior.

Inclusivity and diversity are also critical themes. Effective leaders recognize the value of diverse perspectives and strive to create an inclusive environment where everyone feels valued and respected. For instance, a leader who actively seeks input from team members with different backgrounds and experiences is more likely to foster innovation and creativity. By promoting inclusivity and diversity, leaders can enhance decision-making, improve team performance, and drive organizational success.

Another essential theme is resilience. Leadership often involves navigating setbacks and failures. Resilient leaders can maintain their composure and focus, even in the face of adversity. Consider a leader who remains optimistic and solution-oriented during a major organizational crisis. This leader's resilience not only helps to stabilize the team but also inspires others to persevere. Developing resilience involves cultivating a growth mindset, where challenges are viewed as opportunities for learning and development.

Collaboration and teamwork are also crucial themes. Effective leaders understand that success is rarely achieved in isolation. They prioritize building strong, collaborative teams where members support each other and work towards shared goals. Picture a leader who encourages cross-functional collaboration and fosters a sense of community within the team. This leader's emphasis on teamwork enhances productivity and innovation, as diverse perspectives and skills are brought together to solve complex problems.

Strategic thinking is another key theme. Leaders must be able to think critically and strategically about the long-term direction of their organization. This involves analyzing trends, anticipating challenges, and making informed decisions that align with the organization's goals. Imagine a leader who regularly reviews industry trends and adjusts their strategic plan accordingly. This leader's strategic thinking ensures that the organization remains competitive and well-positioned for future growth.

Finally, continuous learning and development are essential themes in dynamic leadership. Effective leaders are committed to their own growth and the growth of their team members. They prioritize ongoing learning and encourage a culture of continuous improvement. Consider a leader who invests in professional development opportunities for their team and models a commitment to lifelong learning. This leader's focus on development ensures that the team remains adaptable and well-equipped to meet future challenges.

Setting the Stage for Your Leadership Journey

Every leadership journey begins with a single step, but the path to becoming an effective leader requires careful preparation and a strategic mindset. Before diving into the complexities of leading a team or organization, it's crucial to lay a strong foundation. This chapter will guide you through the essential steps to set the stage for your leadership journey, ensuring you embark with clarity, purpose, and confidence.

First and foremost, understanding your personal motivations for pursuing leadership is essential. Reflect on what drives you to lead. Is it a desire to make a positive impact, to innovate, or perhaps to nurture and develop others? Identifying your core motivations will help you stay grounded and focused, especially when facing challenges. Consider the story of Jane, a marketing manager who transitioned into a leadership role. Her primary motivation was to foster a creative environment where her team could thrive. By keeping this motivation at the forefront, she navigated her new responsibilities with authenticity and passion.

Setting clear, achievable goals is another crucial step. Without a roadmap, even the most motivated leaders can lose their way. Start by defining your long-term vision. Where do you see yourself and your team in the next five to ten years? Break this vision down into smaller, actionable goals. For instance, if your long-term vision is to lead a highly innovative team, a short-term goal might be to implement a structured brainstorming process. These smaller goals act as stepping stones, making the larger vision more attainable.

Building self-awareness is a foundational aspect of leadership. Knowing your strengths and weaknesses allows you to leverage your capabilities effectively and seek support where needed. Tools such as the Myers-Briggs Type Indicator (MBTI) or the StrengthsFinder assessment can provide valuable insights into your personality and leadership style. Take the case of John, a CEO who discovered through self-assessment that his strength lay in strategic thinking but he needed to improve his communication skills. Armed with this knowledge, he sought out training and mentorship to enhance his abilities, ultimately becoming a more well-rounded leader.

Developing emotional intelligence (EI) is equally important. EI involves recognizing and managing your own emotions, as well as understanding and influencing the emotions of others. Leaders with high EI are better equipped to handle interpersonal dynamics, resolve conflicts, and inspire their teams. Consider the example of Emma, a team leader who noticed a decline in her team's morale. By using her emotional intelligence, she was able to identify underlying issues, address them empathetically, and restore a positive team atmosphere.

Effective communication is a skill that cannot be overstated in its importance. Leaders must be able to convey their ideas clearly, listen actively, and provide constructive feedback. Practice active listening by giving your full attention to the speaker, asking clarifying questions, and reflecting back what you've heard. This fosters mutual understanding and respect. For example, when Mark, a project manager, started holding regular feedback sessions with his team, he noticed a significant improvement in collaboration and productivity. Clear communication also involves being transparent about decisions and changes, which builds trust and credibility.

Cultivating a growth mindset is vital for continuous improvement. Embrace challenges as opportunities to learn and grow. Encourage your team to adopt the same mindset by celebrating their efforts and resilience, rather than just their successes. Take inspiration from Carol Dweck's research on growth mindset, which shows that individuals who believe their abilities can be developed through dedication and hard work are more likely to achieve higher levels of success. By fostering a culture of continuous learning, you create an environment where innovation and improvement thrive.

Building strong relationships is a cornerstone of effective leadership. Invest time in getting to know your team members, understanding their strengths, aspirations, and concerns. Trust is the foundation of any strong relationship. Demonstrate reliability, show genuine interest in your team's well-being, and be consistent in your actions. Consider the example of Sarah, a department head who made a point to have regular one-on-one meetings with her team members. This not only helped her build rapport but also allowed her to address issues before they escalated.

Adopting a strategic perspective is essential for long-term success. Stay informed about industry trends, competitors, and emerging opportunities. This involves not just looking at the immediate horizon but also considering the broader landscape. Engage in strategic planning sessions and encourage your team to contribute their insights. For instance, Alex, a senior manager, regularly held strategy workshops where team members could brainstorm and discuss market trends. This practice not only generated innovative ideas but also fostered a sense of ownership and alignment with the organization's goals.

Resilience is a trait every leader must develop. The journey will inevitably include setbacks and challenges. Building resilience involves maintaining a positive outlook, staying focused on your goals, and adapting to changing circumstances. Reflect on past experiences where you successfully navigated difficulties and draw strength from those memories. Take the story of Lisa, a startup founder who faced multiple rejections from investors. By staying resilient and continuously refining her pitch, she eventually secured the funding needed to grow her business.

Ethical leadership is about making decisions that are not only effective but also morally sound. Upholding high ethical standards sets a positive example and builds trust within your team and organization. When faced with difficult decisions, consider the long-term implications and whether they align with your values and those of the organization. For example, when David, a company executive, discovered unethical practices within his team, he took immediate action to address the issue, even though it was a challenging and potentially risky move. His commitment to ethics reinforced the company's values and earned him respect.

Finally, fostering inclusivity and diversity within your team is essential for creating a dynamic and innovative environment. Embrace diverse perspectives and create an inclusive culture where everyone feels valued and heard. This can be achieved by actively seeking out diverse candidates during recruitment, promoting open dialogue, and providing equal opportunities for growth and development. Consider the case of Maria, a team leader who implemented a mentorship program that paired employees from different backgrounds. This initiative not only enhanced team cohesion but also sparked creative solutions to complex problems.

Chapter 2

Understanding Dynamic Leadership

Defining Dynamic Leadership

Dynamic leadership is a multifaceted concept that transcends the traditional boundaries of management and authority. It is characterized by the ability to adapt, inspire, and drive change in an ever-evolving environment. To truly understand dynamic leadership, one must delve into its core attributes and the practical ways in which these can be cultivated and applied.

At the heart of dynamic leadership lies adaptability. Leaders who are dynamic possess a keen sense of awareness and the flexibility to pivot when circumstances change. Consider the example of Laura, a director at a tech startup. When a sudden market shift threatened the viability of their flagship product, Laura didn't cling to the original plan. Instead, she rapidly gathered her team, assessed the new landscape, and reallocated resources to a more promising project. Her ability to adapt not only saved the company but also positioned it for future success.

The ability to inspire and motivate is another critical component of dynamic leadership. Leaders who can ignite passion and commitment within their teams often achieve remarkable results. Take the story of Michael, a high school principal who turned around a failing school. By sharing a compelling vision of what the school could become and demonstrating unwavering commitment, he inspired teachers, students, and parents to work together towards this new vision. Michael's dynamic leadership fostered a culture of excellence and collaboration, resulting in improved academic performance and morale.

Effective communication is essential for dynamic leadership. It's not just about conveying information but also about listening, empathizing, and engaging with others. Dynamic leaders excel at understanding the perspectives of their team members and stakeholders. For instance, Rachel, a project manager, faced resistance when introducing a new workflow system. Instead of pushing through her agenda, she organized a series of listening sessions to understand the concerns of her team. This approach allowed her to address their issues and gain their buy-in, ultimately leading to a smoother transition and greater overall satisfaction.

Innovation is another hallmark of dynamic leadership. Leaders who encourage and embrace innovation create environments where creativity and new ideas flourish. Consider the example of Tom, the CEO of a manufacturing company. He implemented an "innovation hour" where employees could work on any project they were passionate about. This initiative led to several breakthrough ideas, including a new product line that significantly boosted the company's revenue. Tom's willingness to foster an innovative culture exemplifies dynamic leadership in action.

Resilience is crucial for dynamic leaders. The ability to bounce back from setbacks and maintain focus on long-term goals differentiates dynamic leaders from others. Look at Jessica, an entrepreneur who faced multiple failures before her company became successful. Each setback was met with determination and a willingness to learn and adapt. Jessica's resilience not only kept her company afloat during tough times but eventually led to its success. Her story demonstrates how dynamic leaders view challenges as opportunities for growth rather than insurmountable obstacles.

Building strong relationships and networks is another defining trait of dynamic leadership. Leaders who understand the value of connections and collaboration are better equipped to navigate the complexities of their roles. For example, David, a nonprofit executive, prioritized building relationships with community leaders, donors, and other organizations. These connections proved invaluable when his organization faced funding cuts. The strong network he had cultivated provided the support needed to secure alternative funding sources and continue their mission.

Emotional intelligence (EI) is a vital attribute for dynamic leaders. Leaders with high EI are adept at managing their own emotions and understanding the emotions of others. This skill allows them to navigate interpersonal dynamics effectively and create a positive work environment. Sarah, a team leader, noticed that her team was struggling with stress during a particularly demanding project. By using her emotional intelligence, she implemented stress-relief activities and provided additional support, which helped her team manage their stress and maintain productivity.

Visionary thinking is integral to dynamic leadership. Leaders with a clear vision of the future can inspire and guide their teams towards long-term goals. They are not just focused on immediate results but also on sustainable growth and development. Consider the example of James, a business leader who envisioned transforming his small local business into a global brand. Through strategic planning and a relentless pursuit of his vision, he successfully expanded his business internationally. James's ability to think beyond the present and plan for the future is a hallmark of dynamic leadership.

Empowerment is a key aspect of dynamic leadership. By empowering team members, leaders foster a sense of ownership and accountability. Empowered employees are more engaged, motivated, and productive. Maria, a department head, implemented a policy of delegating decision-making authority to her team members. This not only allowed them to take on more responsibility but also led to more innovative and effective solutions. Maria's approach demonstrates how dynamic leaders leverage the strengths of their team members to achieve better outcomes.

Self-awareness and continuous learning are essential for dynamic leaders. Leaders who are aware of their strengths and weaknesses can leverage their abilities effectively and seek growth opportunities. Continuous learning ensures that leaders stay relevant and adaptable in a rapidly changing environment. John, a senior manager, regularly sought feedback from his team and participated in professional development programs. This commitment to self-improvement enabled him to lead more effectively and stay ahead in his field.

Ethical leadership is a cornerstone of dynamic leadership. Leaders who prioritize ethics and integrity build trust and credibility with their teams and stakeholders. Ethical behavior sets a positive example and fosters a culture of accountability and transparency. Emma, a corporate executive, faced a situation where she had to choose between short-term profits and long-term sustainability. By making an ethical decision that prioritized sustainability, she reinforced her company's values and earned the respect of her team and customers.

Inclusion and diversity are fundamental to dynamic leadership. Leaders who embrace diverse perspectives and create inclusive environments drive innovation and performance. Inclusive leaders ensure that all voices are heard and valued, leading to better decision-making and outcomes. Alex, a team leader, actively sought to diversify his team and create an inclusive culture. This approach not only enhanced team creativity but also improved overall performance and satisfaction.

The Evolution of Leadership Theories

Leadership theories have evolved significantly over time, reflecting changes in society, organizational structures, and the nature of work itself. Understanding this evolution is crucial for anyone aspiring to become an effective leader, as it provides insights into how leadership has been conceptualized and practiced through different historical contexts and helps in identifying the most relevant and effective approaches for today's dynamic environments.

The earliest theories of leadership, known as trait theories, emerged in the early 20th century. These theories posited that certain individuals are born with innate characteristics that make them natural leaders. Traits such as intelligence, assertiveness, and charisma were considered essential for effective leadership. For instance, Thomas Carlyle's "Great Man Theory" suggested that history is shaped by the actions of extraordinary leaders. Despite its initial popularity, trait theory faced criticism for its inability to explain why some individuals with these traits failed to lead effectively and why successful leaders often displayed vastly different traits.

As the limitations of trait theories became evident, researchers began to focus on behaviors rather than inherent qualities. Behavioral theories of leadership, which gained prominence in the mid-20th century, argued that effective leadership is based on specific behaviors that can be learned and developed. The Ohio State University and University of Michigan studies identified two primary dimensions of leadership behavior: task-oriented behaviors, which focus on achieving goals and organizing work, and people-oriented behaviors, which emphasize building relationships and supporting team members. These studies highlighted that leaders could be trained to adopt behaviors that enhance their effectiveness, marking a significant shift from the idea of inherent traits.

The contingency theories of leadership, which emerged in the 1960s and 1970s, further advanced the understanding of leadership by introducing the idea that the effectiveness of a leader depends on the context or situation. Fred Fiedler's Contingency Model was one of the pioneering frameworks in this category, suggesting that the success of a leader is contingent upon the alignment between their leadership style and the favorableness of the situation. For example, task-oriented leaders might excel in highly structured environments with clear objectives, while relationship-oriented leaders might be more effective in settings that require strong interpersonal dynamics and team cohesion.

Building on the contingency perspective, the Path-Goal Theory, developed by Robert House, proposed that a leader's primary function is to clear the paths to achieve goals by addressing obstacles and providing appropriate support. According to this theory, effective leaders adapt their style to the needs of their team members and the demands of the task. For instance, a leader might adopt a directive style when tasks are ambiguous and require clear guidance, while a supportive style might be more effective when team members are facing stress or uncertainty.

In the late 20th century, transformational and transactional leadership theories gained prominence, offering a more nuanced understanding of leadership dynamics. Transformational leadership, introduced by James MacGregor Burns and later expanded by Bernard Bass, emphasizes the role of leaders in inspiring and motivating their followers to achieve higher levels of performance and personal development. Transformational leaders are characterized by their ability to articulate a compelling vision, foster an environment of trust and creativity, and serve as role models. An example of transformational leadership can be seen in the way Steve Jobs inspired innovation and excellence at Apple by challenging his team to think differently and pursue groundbreaking ideas.

Transactional leadership, on the other hand, is based on a system of rewards and punishments to manage performance. Leaders who adopt this style focus on setting clear goals, monitoring progress, and providing feedback based on performance outcomes. While transactional leadership can be effective in maintaining consistency and achieving short-term objectives, it may not foster the same level of intrinsic motivation and innovation as transformational leadership. However, it is important to note that effective leaders often blend both transformational and transactional approaches depending on the situation and the needs of their organization.

The late 20th and early 21st centuries saw the emergence of new leadership theories that reflect the changing nature of work and organizations. Servant leadership, popularized by Robert Greenleaf, emphasizes the leader's role as a servant to their followers. This approach prioritizes the well-being and development of team members, fostering a culture of trust, empathy, and collaboration. Servant leaders focus on empowering their followers, helping them grow, and ensuring their needs are met. An example of servant leadership can be seen in organizations like Southwest Airlines, where leaders prioritize employee satisfaction and engagement, resulting in high levels of customer service and organizational performance.

Another contemporary approach is authentic leadership, which emphasizes the importance of self-awareness, transparency, and ethical behavior. Authentic leaders are genuine and lead with integrity, building trust and credibility with their followers. They are consistent in their actions and words, fostering an environment of openness and honesty. Authentic leadership is particularly relevant in today's context, where stakeholders increasingly demand ethical conduct and accountability from organizational leaders. For instance, Howard Schultz, former CEO of Starbucks, is often cited as an authentic leader for his commitment to ethical business practices and social responsibility.

Distributed leadership, also known as shared leadership, is another modern theory that recognizes the complexity of contemporary organizations. This approach suggests that leadership is not confined to a single individual but is distributed across various members of the organization. It emphasizes collaboration, collective decision-making, and the utilization of diverse expertise within the team. Distributed leadership is particularly effective in knowledge-based and innovative environments, where the complexity of tasks requires input from multiple individuals. An example of distributed leadership can be seen in agile software development teams, where leadership responsibilities are shared among team members to foster creativity and responsiveness.

Charismatic leadership, which intersects with transformational leadership, focuses on the personal charm and influence of the leader. Charismatic leaders inspire and captivate their followers through their vision, communication skills, and personal magnetism. They often emerge in times of crisis or significant change, rallying people around a common cause. However, while charismatic leadership can be powerful, it also carries risks if the leader's influence is misused or if followers become overly dependent on their charisma.

Characteristics of Dynamic Leaders

Dynamic leaders possess a unique blend of qualities that enable them to inspire, motivate, and guide their teams through change and uncertainty. They are not confined to a single style or approach but adapt their behavior to meet the demands of different situations and the needs of their followers. Understanding these characteristics can provide valuable insights for anyone aspiring to become a more effective leader in today's fast-paced and ever-changing world.

At the heart of dynamic leadership lies the ability to communicate effectively. Dynamic leaders are exceptional communicators who can articulate their vision and goals with clarity and passion. They use storytelling to connect with their audience, making their messages more memorable and impactful. For instance, consider how Martin Luther King Jr. used his "I Have a Dream" speech to paint a vivid picture of a better future, inspiring millions to join the civil rights movement. By conveying their vision in a compelling way, dynamic leaders align their teams towards common goals and foster a sense of purpose.

Adaptability is another crucial trait of dynamic leaders. In an environment where change is the only constant, the ability to pivot and adjust strategies is invaluable. Dynamic leaders are not rigid in their thinking; they embrace flexibility and are open to new ideas and approaches. They are quick to recognize when a plan is not working and are willing to course-correct to navigate obstacles and seize opportunities. This adaptability extends to their leadership style as well. They understand that different situations and team members require different approaches, and they tailor their leadership to meet these varying needs.

Empathy is a distinguishing feature of dynamic leaders. They possess a deep understanding of their team members' emotions, motivations, and challenges. This emotional intelligence enables them to build strong relationships and create a supportive and inclusive environment. Empathetic leaders listen actively and show genuine concern for their team's well-being. They recognize and value the diverse perspectives and experiences that each team member brings, fostering a culture of respect and collaboration. This, in turn, enhances team cohesion and drives better performance.

Visionary thinking sets dynamic leaders apart. They have a clear and compelling vision for the future and are able to inspire others to share in that vision. This forward-thinking mindset allows them to anticipate trends and stay ahead of the curve. They are not content with maintaining the status quo but are constantly seeking ways to innovate and improve. Visionary leaders challenge their teams to think creatively and push the boundaries of what is possible. By setting ambitious goals and encouraging a culture of continuous improvement, they drive progress and achievement.

Resilience is a key attribute of dynamic leaders. They possess the mental toughness to persevere through setbacks and challenges. Rather than being discouraged by failure, they view it as an opportunity to learn and grow. This resilience enables them to maintain a positive and proactive attitude, even in the face of adversity. Their ability to stay calm under pressure and maintain focus on their goals provides stability and reassurance to their teams. Resilient leaders inspire confidence and demonstrate that challenges can be overcome with determination and perseverance.

Authenticity is another hallmark of dynamic leaders. They lead with integrity and are true to their values and principles. Authentic leaders are transparent and honest in their interactions, building trust and credibility with their teams. They do not try to project a false image or conform to others' expectations but remain genuine and consistent in their actions and decisions. This authenticity fosters a culture of trust and openness, where team members feel safe to express their ideas and concerns. By leading by example, authentic leaders encourage others to act with integrity and accountability.

Dynamic leaders also possess a strong sense of accountability. They take responsibility for their actions and decisions and hold themselves and their teams to high standards. They set clear expectations and provide the necessary support and resources to achieve them. When things go wrong, they do not shift blame but address issues head-on and work towards solutions. This accountability creates a culture of ownership and empowerment, where team members feel a sense of responsibility for their contributions and are motivated to perform at their best.

Another critical characteristic of dynamic leaders is their ability to build and nurture high-performing teams. They understand that success is not achieved in isolation but through the collective efforts of a motivated and engaged team. Dynamic leaders invest time and effort in developing their team members, providing opportunities for growth and learning. They recognize and celebrate individual and team achievements, fostering a sense of pride and accomplishment. By creating an environment where team members feel valued and supported, dynamic leaders cultivate loyalty and commitment.

Strategic thinking is essential for dynamic leaders. They are able to see the big picture and make decisions that align with long-term goals. Strategic leaders are adept at analyzing complex situations, identifying key drivers, and developing plans that leverage strengths and mitigate risks. They are proactive in seeking out new opportunities and are not afraid to take calculated risks to achieve their objectives. This strategic mindset enables them to navigate uncertainty and guide their teams towards sustainable success.

Finally, dynamic leaders are lifelong learners. They have a growth mindset and are committed to continuous personal and professional development. They stay curious and seek out new knowledge and experiences to enhance their skills and understanding. Dynamic leaders are open to feedback and use it as a tool for improvement. They encourage a culture of learning within their teams, promoting innovation and adaptability. By staying ahead of the curve and fostering a learning-oriented environment, dynamic leaders ensure that their teams remain competitive and resilient in a rapidly changing world.

The Impact of Dynamic Leadership on Organizations

Dynamic leadership significantly influences organizational success, shaping not only how teams perform but also how they adapt to change, innovate, and achieve long-term goals. The impact of dynamic leaders is profound and multifaceted, affecting everything from employee morale and productivity to organizational culture and strategic direction.

Dynamic leaders excel in fostering a culture of innovation. By encouraging creativity and risk-taking, they enable their teams to explore new ideas and solutions. This innovation culture is essential in today's rapidly changing business environment, where staying ahead of the curve often determines success or failure. For instance, consider how Elon Musk's leadership at Tesla has driven the company to the forefront of electric vehicle technology. His willingness to challenge conventional thinking and support groundbreaking ideas has propelled Tesla to become a leader in sustainable energy solutions.

A hallmark of dynamic leadership is the ability to inspire and motivate employees. Dynamic leaders connect with their teams on a personal level, understanding their individual strengths, aspirations, and concerns. This connection fosters a sense of belonging and purpose, driving higher levels of engagement and commitment. When employees feel valued and inspired, they are more likely to go above and beyond in their roles. This increased engagement translates to higher productivity, better customer service, and improved overall performance. For example, Howard Schultz's leadership at Starbucks cultivated a strong organizational culture that prioritized employee satisfaction, resulting in loyal and motivated staff who contributed to the company's growth and success.

Dynamic leaders also play a critical role in navigating organizations through periods of change and uncertainty. Their ability to adapt and remain flexible is crucial in times of crisis or transition. By maintaining a clear vision and providing steady guidance, they help their teams stay focused and resilient. This stability is vital for sustaining performance and morale during challenging times. Dynamic leaders ensure that their organizations are agile and responsive, capable of adjusting strategies and operations to meet evolving market demands. During the COVID-19 pandemic, many leaders demonstrated dynamic leadership by swiftly adapting business models, implementing remote work policies, and finding new ways to serve customers, thereby ensuring business continuity and survival.

Employee development is another area where dynamic leadership has a significant impact. Dynamic leaders invest in the growth and development of their team members, recognizing that their success is intertwined with the organization's success. They provide opportunities for continuous learning, mentorship, and career advancement. This commitment to development not only enhances individual capabilities but also builds a more skilled and versatile workforce. Companies led by dynamic leaders often see higher retention rates, as employees are more likely to stay with organizations that invest in their professional growth. For instance, companies like Google and Amazon are known for their commitment to employee development, offering extensive training programs and clear career progression paths, which contribute to their status as top employers.

The influence of dynamic leadership extends to organizational culture. Leaders set the tone for the values, behaviors, and norms that define an organization. Dynamic leaders cultivate an inclusive and collaborative culture where diverse perspectives are valued, and teamwork is encouraged. This positive culture fosters innovation, enhances problem-solving capabilities, and creates a supportive environment where employees can thrive. A strong, positive culture also attracts top talent, further strengthening the organization. Consider the example of Patagonia, where dynamic leadership has created a culture centered on environmental sustainability and employee well-being, attracting individuals who are passionate about making a positive impact.

Strategic vision is another critical aspect impacted by dynamic leadership. Dynamic leaders possess the foresight to anticipate future trends and challenges, enabling them to set strategic directions that position their organizations for long-term success. They are not only focused on immediate results but also on building sustainable growth and competitiveness. This strategic vision guides decision-making at all levels, ensuring that actions align with the organization's long-term goals. Dynamic leaders balance short-term objectives with long-term ambitions, creating a roadmap that navigates the complexities of the business landscape. For example, Satya Nadella's leadership at Microsoft has been characterized by a forward-thinking vision that has driven the company's transformation into a cloud computing leader, ensuring its relevance and growth in the digital age.

Dynamic leadership also enhances organizational resilience. Leaders who demonstrate resilience in the face of challenges inspire their teams to do the same. They model perseverance and a positive attitude, which are crucial for maintaining morale and momentum during difficult times. This resilience permeates the organization, creating a culture that views setbacks as opportunities for learning and growth rather than insurmountable obstacles. Organizations led by resilient leaders are better equipped to handle crises, bounce back from failures, and emerge stronger. The turnaround stories of companies like IBM and Ford, which faced significant challenges but rebounded under dynamic leadership, highlight the importance of resilience in achieving long-term success.

Another significant impact of dynamic leadership is the ability to build and maintain strong stakeholder relationships. Dynamic leaders understand the importance of engaging with stakeholders, including customers, partners, investors, and the community. They prioritize transparency, communication, and mutual respect in these relationships, fostering trust and collaboration. Strong stakeholder relationships are essential for securing support, resources, and opportunities that drive organizational growth and success. Leaders who actively engage with stakeholders and address their needs build a loyal and supportive network that contributes to the organization's stability and reputation. For example, companies with strong customer relationships often see higher levels of customer loyalty and advocacy, which are critical for sustained business success.

Dynamic leadership also influences the ethical standards and social responsibility of an organization. Leaders who prioritize ethical behavior and social responsibility set a powerful example for their teams and the broader organization. They ensure that business practices align with ethical principles and contribute positively to society. This commitment to ethics and social responsibility enhances the organization's reputation, builds trust with stakeholders, and can even drive business performance. Companies known for their ethical leadership, such as Ben & Jerry's and The Body Shop, have built strong brands and loyal customer bases by demonstrating a commitment to social and environmental causes.

Case Studies of Dynamic Leaders

Steve Jobs' transformative journey with Apple Inc. offers a quintessential example of dynamic leadership. Jobs returned to Apple in 1997, a company he co-founded but was ousted from in 1985. At that time, Apple was struggling, teetering on the brink of bankruptcy. Jobs' dynamic leadership was pivotal in reinventing Apple into one of the most valuable companies in the world. His ability to envision the future of technology and consumer electronics drove Apple to innovate with products like the iPod, iPhone, and iPad. Jobs' insistence on simplicity and elegance in design, coupled with a relentless focus on user experience, set new industry standards. His leadership style, characterized by a blend of visionary thinking, attention to detail, and a demanding nature, created a culture of excellence and innovation. Under Jobs, Apple didn't just build products; it built a brand synonymous with quality and cutting-edge technology.

Another compelling case of dynamic leadership is seen in the tenure of Indra Nooyi at PepsiCo. Nooyi, who served as CEO from 2006 to 2018, transformed the company with her strategic vision and emphasis on sustainability. Her leadership was marked by a clear focus on long-term growth and innovation. Nooyi launched the "Performance with Purpose" initiative, which aimed to deliver sustainable growth by investing in a healthier future for people and our planet. This strategy involved diversifying PepsiCo's product portfolio to include healthier options, reducing the environmental impact of the company's operations, and fostering an inclusive company culture. Nooyi's ability to foresee consumer trends towards healthier lifestyles and sustainability helped PepsiCo adapt and thrive in a changing market. Her leadership demonstrated how a clear, purpose-driven vision could drive both business success and positive societal impact.

Satya Nadella's leadership at Microsoft provides another illuminating example. Taking over as CEO in 2014, Nadella inherited a company that was struggling to find its footing in a rapidly evolving tech landscape. His dynamic leadership has been instrumental in revitalizing Microsoft. Nadella shifted the company's focus to cloud computing, leading the transformation with the Azure cloud platform. He also fostered a culture of collaboration and innovation, breaking down silos within the company and encouraging a growth mindset among employees. Nadella's emphasis on empathy and learning has reshaped Microsoft's corporate culture, making it more inclusive and adaptable. His strategic vision and ability to inspire and mobilize his workforce have driven Microsoft to new heights, making it one of the most valuable companies globally.

Mary Barra's ascent to the CEO position at General Motors (GM) in 2014 marked a significant moment in the automotive industry. Barra, the first female CEO of a major global automaker, faced numerous challenges, including a massive vehicle recall and the need to steer the company towards a more sustainable future. Her dynamic leadership has been characterized by a commitment to transparency, accountability, and innovation. Barra has focused on transforming GM into a leader in electric and autonomous vehicles, setting ambitious goals for the company's future. Under her leadership, GM has made significant investments in electric vehicle technology and announced plans to phase out gasoline and diesel-powered cars by 2035. Barra's ability to navigate crises, drive innovation, and maintain a clear strategic vision has positioned GM as a forward-thinking leader in the automotive industry.

The leadership of Reed Hastings at Netflix offers another compelling case study. Hastings co-founded Netflix in 1997, and his dynamic leadership has been crucial in the company's evolution from a DVD rental service to a global streaming giant. Hastings' willingness to embrace change and disrupt existing business models has been key to Netflix's success. He recognized early on the potential of streaming technology and invested heavily in developing a streaming platform, even at the risk of cannibalizing Netflix's DVD rental business. This bold move paid off, positioning Netflix as a pioneer in the streaming industry. Hastings also fostered a culture of innovation and creativity at Netflix, encouraging employees to take risks and experiment with new ideas. His leadership has enabled Netflix to continually adapt to changing market dynamics and consumer preferences, maintaining its position as a leader in the entertainment industry.

A further example of dynamic leadership is Jeff Bezos' tenure at Amazon. Bezos founded Amazon in 1994 as an online bookstore and transformed it into one of the largest and most diverse e-commerce businesses in the world. His dynamic leadership has been characterized by a relentless focus on customer satisfaction, innovation, and long-term thinking. Bezos' willingness to invest in new technologies and business models, such as Amazon Web Services (AWS), has been instrumental in Amazon's growth. AWS has become a significant revenue driver for the company, showcasing Bezos' ability to foresee and capitalize on emerging trends. His leadership style, which emphasizes experimentation, failure tolerance, and continuous improvement, has created a culture of innovation at Amazon. Bezos' strategic vision and dynamic leadership have made Amazon a dominant force in multiple industries, from retail to cloud computing.

Reflecting on these case studies, it becomes clear that dynamic leadership is not confined to a single industry or leadership style. Whether it's Jobs' visionary approach, Nooyi's purpose-driven strategy, Nadella's empathetic transformation, Barra's crisis management and innovation, Hastings' disruptive mindset, or Bezos' relentless focus on customer satisfaction, each leader demonstrates unique ways to drive organizational success. What unites them is their ability to adapt, inspire, and lead their organizations through change and uncertainty.

Dynamic leaders possess a deep understanding of their industries and an unwavering commitment to their vision. They are not afraid to take risks or make bold decisions that challenge the status quo. Their leadership fosters a culture of innovation, resilience, and continuous improvement, enabling their organizations to thrive in a rapidly changing world. Aspiring leaders can learn valuable lessons from these examples, understanding that dynamic leadership requires a balance of strategic vision, emotional intelligence, and the ability to inspire and mobilize teams towards common goals.

Chapter 3

Developing Self-Awareness

The Role of Self-Awareness in Leadership

Self-awareness is the cornerstone of effective leadership, acting as a compass that guides leaders toward better decision-making, stronger relationships, and more resilient organizations. Understanding oneself—one's strengths, weaknesses, values, and impact on others—enables leaders to navigate the complexities of leadership with clarity and confidence. This chapter delves into the multifaceted role of self-awareness in leadership, examining how it influences various aspects of a leader's journey and offering practical insights for developing and enhancing this critical trait.

Self-awareness begins with an honest assessment of one's strengths and weaknesses. Leaders who are aware of their capabilities can leverage their strengths to inspire and drive their teams, while also recognizing areas where they need support or development. This balance prevents overconfidence and allows for a more realistic approach to challenges. For instance, a leader who excels in strategic thinking but struggles with interpersonal communication might focus on building a team that complements these skills, ensuring that the organization benefits from a well-rounded leadership approach.

The ability to understand and regulate one's emotions is another crucial component of self-awareness. Emotional intelligence, or the ability to perceive, interpret, and manage emotions, is deeply rooted in self-awareness. Leaders who are attuned to their emotional responses can maintain composure under pressure, make rational decisions, and communicate effectively. This emotional stability fosters trust and respect among team members, creating a positive work environment. For example, a leader who can remain calm and composed during a crisis will likely instill confidence in their team, guiding them through turbulent times with a steady hand.

Self-awareness also plays a pivotal role in shaping a leader's values and ethical framework. Leaders who are clear about their core values can align their actions and decisions with these principles, ensuring consistency and integrity in their leadership. This alignment not only enhances personal credibility but also sets a powerful example for others to follow. When leaders demonstrate a commitment to their values, they create a culture of trust and accountability within the organization. Consider a leader who prioritizes transparency and open communication; their actions will encourage a culture where employees feel valued and heard, leading to higher engagement and morale.

Understanding one's impact on others is another critical aspect of self-awareness. Leaders who are aware of how their behavior affects their team can adjust their approach to foster positive interactions and outcomes. This awareness involves recognizing both the intended and unintended consequences of one's actions. For instance, a leader who frequently interrupts during meetings might unintentionally stifle open communication and creativity. By becoming aware of this behavior, the leader can consciously make an effort to listen more actively, thereby encouraging more participation and collaboration.

Self-awareness also enhances a leader's ability to give and receive feedback. Leaders who are open to feedback demonstrate humility and a willingness to grow, which can inspire the same attitude in their team members. Constructive feedback, when delivered with empathy and understanding, can lead to significant personal and professional development. Additionally, self-aware leaders can provide more meaningful and impactful feedback to their teams, helping individuals to improve and succeed. For example, a leader who understands their own communication style can tailor their feedback to suit the recipient's preferences, making the feedback more effective and easier to act upon.

Developing self-awareness is an ongoing process that requires intentional effort and reflection. One effective method is through regular self-reflection, where leaders take time to evaluate their actions, decisions, and interactions. This practice can involve journaling, meditating, or simply taking quiet moments to think. Reflecting on past experiences allows leaders to learn from their successes and mistakes, fostering continuous improvement. Another valuable approach is seeking feedback from others, such as peers, mentors, or team members. Honest feedback provides external perspectives that can highlight blind spots and offer insights that might not be apparent from self-reflection alone.

Self-awareness also benefits from structured assessments, such as personality tests or 360-degree feedback tools. These assessments provide a comprehensive view of a leader's strengths, weaknesses, and behavioral tendencies, offering a foundation for targeted development. For instance, tools like the Myers-Briggs Type Indicator (MBTI) or the Emotional Intelligence Quotient (EQ-i) can provide valuable insights into a leader's personality traits and emotional competencies. Armed with this knowledge, leaders can create personalized development plans to enhance their self-awareness and overall effectiveness.

Incorporating mindfulness practices into daily routines can further enhance self-awareness. Mindfulness involves being fully present and engaged in the current moment, without judgment. This practice helps leaders to stay attuned to their thoughts, emotions, and physical sensations, fostering a deeper understanding of their inner experiences. Mindfulness can also reduce stress and improve focus, contributing to better decision-making and leadership performance. For example, a leader who practices mindfulness might be more adept at noticing their emotional triggers and managing their responses, leading to more thoughtful and measured interactions with their team.

Mentorship and coaching are also powerful tools for developing self-awareness. Engaging with a mentor or coach provides leaders with guidance, support, and constructive feedback. These relationships offer a safe space for leaders to explore their self-awareness journey, gain new perspectives, and develop strategies for growth. Mentors and coaches can help leaders to identify and challenge limiting beliefs, set meaningful goals, and navigate complex situations with greater clarity and confidence. For instance, a coach might help a leader to uncover underlying fears or insecurities that impact their leadership style, enabling them to address these issues and lead more effectively.

Ultimately, self-awareness is not just about understanding oneself; it also involves understanding others and the broader context in which one operates. Leaders who are self-aware are better equipped to empathize with their team members, appreciate diverse perspectives, and navigate organizational dynamics. This broader awareness enhances a leader's ability to build strong, collaborative relationships and foster a positive organizational culture. For example, a self-aware leader who understands the cultural nuances of their team can create an inclusive environment that values and leverages diversity, leading to greater innovation and engagement.

Tools for Self-Assessment

Understanding oneself is a journey that can be both enlightening and challenging. To navigate this path effectively, individuals can employ various self-assessment tools. These tools provide a structured approach to introspection, helping to uncover strengths, weaknesses, preferences, and areas for development. By leveraging these tools, one can gain deeper insights into their personality, behaviors, and potential, ultimately leading to more informed decisions and personal growth.

One of the most widely recognized self-assessment tools is the Myers-Briggs Type Indicator (MBTI). This tool categorizes individuals into 16 distinct personality types based on preferences in four dichotomies: Extraversion (E) vs. Introversion (I), Sensing (S) vs. Intuition (N), Thinking (T) vs. Feeling (F), and Judging (J) vs. Perceiving (P). By understanding their MBTI type, individuals can gain insights into their natural tendencies, communication styles, and decision-making processes. For example, an individual identified as an INTJ might recognize their strengths in strategic thinking and long-term planning, while also acknowledging a potential need to improve interpersonal skills.

Another valuable tool is the CliftonStrengths assessment, formerly known as StrengthsFinder. This tool focuses on identifying and developing one's natural talents. Participants receive a detailed report outlining their top strengths, along with strategies to leverage these strengths in various aspects of life. By concentrating on what they do best, individuals can enhance their performance, increase their engagement, and achieve greater satisfaction in their personal and professional endeavors. For instance, someone with the strength of "Learner" might pursue continuous education and skill development, thriving in environments that offer opportunities for growth and exploration.

The Big Five Personality Test, or the Five-Factor Model, is another robust self-assessment tool that measures five core dimensions of personality: Openness to Experience, Conscientiousness, Extraversion, Agreeableness, and Neuroticism. This model provides a comprehensive overview of an individual's personality traits, which can be useful in understanding how they interact with the world around them. For example, high scores in Openness to Experience might indicate a propensity for creativity and curiosity, while high Conscientiousness could suggest a strong sense of responsibility and organization.

Emotional intelligence (EI) assessments, such as the Emotional Quotient Inventory (EQ-i), are designed to evaluate one's ability to recognize, understand, and manage their own emotions and those of others. High emotional intelligence is associated with better interpersonal relationships, effective communication, and resilience under stress. By understanding their EI scores, individuals can identify areas for improvement, such as empathy or emotional regulation, and work on developing these skills. For example, someone with a lower score in emotional self-awareness might practice mindfulness techniques to become more attuned to their emotional states and triggers.

The DISC assessment is another popular tool that categorizes behavior into four primary types: Dominance, Influence, Steadiness, and Conscientiousness. This tool helps individuals understand their behavior patterns, communication styles, and how they approach tasks and challenges. For instance, a person with a high Dominance score might be assertive and results-oriented, while someone with a high Steadiness score might prioritize harmony and consistency. By recognizing these traits, individuals can adapt their approaches to better collaborate with others and achieve their goals.

Self-assessment is not limited to personality and behavior; it also extends to skills and competencies. Tools like the Skills Development Inventory (SDI) help individuals evaluate their proficiency in various skills, from technical abilities to soft skills like leadership and teamwork. By identifying skill gaps, individuals can create targeted development plans to enhance their capabilities. For example, an aspiring manager might use an SDI to assess their leadership skills, identifying areas such as conflict resolution or strategic planning that require further development.

The Values in Action (VIA) Classification of Character Strengths is another insightful tool that focuses on identifying and nurturing one's core virtues and character strengths. This tool categorizes strengths into six broad areas: wisdom, courage, humanity, justice, temperance, and transcendence. By understanding their top character strengths, individuals can align their actions with their values, leading to a more fulfilling and authentic life. For instance, someone with a strength in "Gratitude" might actively practice expressing appreciation, enhancing their overall well-being and relationships.

Regular self-reflection is a critical component of effective self-assessment. Journaling is a powerful practice that allows individuals to document their thoughts, feelings, and experiences, providing a space for introspection and growth. By regularly writing about their experiences, individuals can identify patterns, gain insights into their behaviors, and track their progress over time. For example, journaling about daily interactions can help someone recognize recurring challenges in communication, prompting them to seek strategies for improvement.

Feedback from others is another invaluable resource in the self-assessment process. Seeking input from colleagues, mentors, and peers provides external perspectives that can highlight blind spots and offer constructive insights. Tools like 360-degree feedback assessments gather feedback from multiple sources, offering a comprehensive view of one's performance and behavior. By embracing this feedback, individuals can gain a more accurate understanding of their strengths and areas for development. For example, feedback from team members might reveal a tendency to micromanage, prompting a leader to work on delegating more effectively.

Mindfulness and meditation practices also contribute significantly to self-assessment. These practices encourage individuals to focus on the present moment, fostering greater awareness of their thoughts, emotions, and physical sensations. By cultivating mindfulness, individuals can become more attuned to their inner experiences, enhancing their self-awareness and emotional regulation. For example, a daily meditation practice might help someone recognize stress triggers and develop healthier coping mechanisms.

Mentorship and coaching relationships provide personalized guidance and support in the self-assessment journey. Engaging with a mentor or coach allows individuals to explore their strengths, weaknesses, and goals in a structured and supportive environment. These relationships offer valuable insights, accountability, and encouragement, helping individuals navigate their personal and professional development. For instance, a coach might help a client set specific, measurable goals for improving their leadership skills, providing ongoing feedback and support as they work towards these objectives.

Incorporating self-assessment tools into daily routines requires commitment and intentionality. Setting aside regular time for reflection, whether through journaling, meditation, or seeking feedback, ensures that self-assessment becomes an integral part of one's growth journey. By consistently engaging with these tools, individuals can maintain a clear understanding of their progress, make informed decisions, and continuously evolve.

Identifying Strengths and Weaknesses

Discovering one's strengths and weaknesses is a crucial step in personal and professional development. This process requires introspection, honest evaluation, and sometimes a bit of external feedback. By identifying what you excel at and where you might need improvement, you can create a roadmap for growth that leverages your strengths and addresses your weaknesses.

A practical first step in identifying strengths and weaknesses is self-reflection. Taking time to think about past experiences, both successes and failures, can provide valuable insights. Reflect on moments when you felt particularly effective or when tasks seemed to come naturally. These moments often highlight your strengths. Conversely, consider situations where you struggled or felt out of your depth. These instances can reveal areas where you might need to improve.

Another effective method for self-assessment is keeping a journal. Regularly documenting your thoughts, feelings, and experiences allows you to track patterns over time. For instance, you might notice recurring themes of success in teamwork or problem-solving, indicating strengths in those areas. On the other hand, frequent challenges with time management or communication might point to weaknesses that need addressing.

Soliciting feedback from others is also invaluable. Colleagues, mentors, and friends can offer perspectives that you might not see yourself. Engaging in open and honest conversations about your performance and behaviors can uncover blind spots. For example, a mentor might observe that you excel in strategic thinking but often overlook details, providing a balanced view of your strengths and weaknesses.

Formal assessments, such as personality tests and skills inventories, can provide structured insights. Tools like the Myers-Briggs Type Indicator (MBTI) or the CliftonStrengths assessment categorize personality traits and strengths, offering detailed reports that highlight your natural tendencies. These assessments are based on extensive research and can provide a comprehensive view of your capabilities and areas for growth.

Consider the feedback you receive from performance reviews at work. These reviews are designed to evaluate your contributions and highlight both your strengths and areas needing improvement. Pay close attention to recurring themes in this feedback. Consistent praise for leadership skills or technical proficiency points to strengths, while repeated suggestions for improving delegation or time management indicate weaknesses.

Engaging in new and diverse experiences can also help identify strengths and weaknesses. Stepping out of your comfort zone and trying different roles or tasks can reveal hidden talents or challenges. For instance, volunteering for a project management role might uncover your ability to lead and organize, while also highlighting a need to develop better stress management techniques.

Once you have identified your strengths, it is important to leverage them effectively. Strengths are not just skills you are good at; they are areas that energize and motivate you. By focusing on these areas, you can maximize your impact and satisfaction. For example, if you discover a strength in creative problem-solving, seek opportunities to engage in tasks that require innovative thinking. This not only enhances your performance but also keeps you engaged and motivated.

Addressing weaknesses, on the other hand, requires a strategic approach. It is important to recognize that everyone has weaknesses, and acknowledging them is the first step towards improvement. Developing a plan to address these areas can involve setting specific, measurable goals. For instance, if you struggle with public speaking, you might set a goal to practice by presenting in smaller, less intimidating settings before gradually increasing the audience size.

Seeking out resources to improve weaknesses is also crucial. This might involve taking courses, reading books, or finding a mentor with expertise in the area you want to develop. For example, if you need to improve your time management skills, enrolling in a workshop or reading a highly recommended book on the subject can provide practical strategies and tools.

Another effective strategy is to build a support network. Surrounding yourself with people who complement your weaknesses can create a balanced team dynamic. For example, if you are strong in big-picture thinking but weak in detail orientation, partnering with someone who excels in attention to detail can enhance overall performance. This approach not only addresses weaknesses but also fosters collaboration and mutual growth.

It is also important to practice self-compassion while working on weaknesses. Improvement takes time and effort, and setbacks are a natural part of the process. Being kind to yourself and maintaining a growth mindset can help you stay motivated and resilient. For example, if you miss a goal, instead of being overly critical, analyze what went wrong and adjust your approach accordingly.

Regularly revisiting and reassessing your strengths and weaknesses is essential for continuous growth. As you progress in your personal and professional life, your strengths can evolve, and new weaknesses might emerge. Periodic self-assessment ensures that you remain aware of these changes and can adapt your development strategies accordingly. For instance, a strength in technical skills might become less relevant as you move into a leadership role, requiring you to develop new strengths in management and interpersonal communication.

Incorporating feedback loops into your routine can aid in this ongoing assessment. Regular check-ins with mentors, supervisors, or peers can provide fresh insights and keep you aligned with your development goals. For example, setting up quarterly meetings with a mentor to discuss progress and challenges can ensure that you stay on track and adjust your plans as needed.

Ultimately, identifying strengths and weaknesses is not just about self-improvement; it is about creating a balanced and fulfilling life. By understanding and leveraging your strengths, you can pursue opportunities that align with your passions and talents. Addressing weaknesses ensures that you continue to grow and adapt, enhancing your overall effectiveness and satisfaction. This balance is key to navigating the complexities of both personal and professional landscapes.

Emotional Intelligence and Leadership

Emotional intelligence (EI) has emerged as a critical skill for effective leadership. It encompasses the ability to recognize, understand, and manage our own emotions, as well as the capacity to recognize, understand, and influence the emotions of others. Leaders with high emotional intelligence can navigate the complex social dynamics of the workplace, inspire and motivate their teams, and foster a positive organizational culture.

One of the core components of emotional intelligence is self-awareness. This involves understanding your own emotions, strengths, weaknesses, values, and drivers. For leaders, self-awareness is crucial because it helps them remain grounded and authentic. A self-aware leader can recognize when their emotions are influencing their decisions and actions, allowing them to respond more thoughtfully rather than react impulsively. For example, a leader who understands that they tend to become anxious under pressure can take proactive steps to manage their stress, ensuring it does not negatively impact their team.

Self-regulation, another key aspect of emotional intelligence, refers to the ability to control or redirect disruptive emotions and impulses. Leaders who can self-regulate are able to maintain their composure, even in challenging situations. This stability fosters a sense of trust and dependability among team members. Imagine a scenario where a critical project faces unexpected setbacks. A leader who remains calm and composed can effectively communicate the situation, reassess the plan, and guide the team through the crisis without escalating tensions or causing panic.

Motivation, driven by emotional intelligence, goes beyond external rewards and focuses on intrinsic desires to achieve goals and pursue excellence. Leaders with high motivation are passionate about their work and inspire the same level of enthusiasm in their teams. They set high standards, demonstrate resilience in the face of obstacles, and maintain a positive outlook. For instance, a leader who consistently shows enthusiasm and dedication can ignite a similar drive in their team, leading to increased productivity and a stronger commitment to shared objectives.

Empathy is the ability to understand and share the feelings of others, and it is a fundamental component of emotional intelligence. Empathetic leaders can connect with their team members on a deeper level, fostering strong relationships and a supportive work environment. They listen actively, show genuine concern for others' well-being, and are adept at handling interpersonal conflicts. For example, when a team member is struggling with personal issues, an empathetic leader can offer support and flexibility, which not only helps the individual but also strengthens team cohesion and loyalty.

Social skills, the final pillar of emotional intelligence, involve the ability to manage relationships and build networks. Leaders with strong social skills are effective communicators, adept at conflict resolution, and skilled at fostering collaboration. They can influence and inspire others, leading to more cohesive and high-performing teams. Consider a leader who excels at facilitating open dialogue and encouraging diverse perspectives. This inclusive approach not only enhances problem-solving and innovation but also creates a culture where team members feel valued and empowered.

Developing emotional intelligence is an ongoing process that requires intentional practice and reflection. Leaders can start by seeking feedback from trusted colleagues and mentors to gain insights into their emotional strengths and areas for improvement. Regularly reflecting on their emotional responses and the impact of their behavior on others can also foster greater self-awareness and self-regulation.

Leaders can enhance their empathy and social skills by actively engaging with their team members. This might involve setting aside time for one-on-one meetings, where they can listen to concerns, provide support, and build stronger connections. Additionally, leaders can participate in team-building activities and social events to foster a sense of camaraderie and trust.

Another effective strategy for developing emotional intelligence is mindfulness practice. Mindfulness involves paying attention to the present moment without judgment. By practicing mindfulness, leaders can become more aware of their emotional states and responses, allowing them to manage stress and make more thoughtful decisions. Techniques such as meditation, deep breathing exercises, and mindful observation can help leaders cultivate a greater sense of calm and clarity.

Leadership training programs that focus on emotional intelligence can also be beneficial. These programs often include workshops, coaching, and peer-to-peer learning opportunities that provide leaders with the tools and techniques needed to enhance their emotional intelligence. For instance, role-playing exercises can help leaders practice empathy and active listening, while group discussions can provide insights into managing emotions and building effective relationships.

The benefits of emotional intelligence in leadership extend beyond individual performance to influence organizational success. Leaders with high emotional intelligence can create a positive organizational culture characterized by trust, collaboration, and mutual respect. This culture not only enhances employee satisfaction and retention but also drives innovation and productivity.

Consider a company where the leadership team prioritizes emotional intelligence. Employees in such an environment are likely to feel more valued and supported, leading to higher levels of engagement and motivation. This, in turn, can result in lower turnover rates, as employees are more likely to stay with an organization that recognizes and nurtures their emotional and professional needs.

Moreover, organizations led by emotionally intelligent leaders are better equipped to navigate change and uncertainty. In today's rapidly evolving business landscape, the ability to manage emotions and maintain strong relationships is crucial for adapting to new challenges and seizing opportunities. Leaders who can inspire confidence and resilience in their teams are more likely to drive successful change initiatives and sustain long-term growth.

Continuous Self-Improvement

Continuous self-improvement is the cornerstone of personal and professional growth. It involves a commitment to lifelong learning and development, embracing the mindset that one can always evolve and enhance their skills, knowledge, and character. This journey is not about perfection but about progress, and it requires a strategic approach, resilience, and a willingness to step out of one's comfort zone.

The first step in continuous self-improvement is setting clear, achievable goals. Goals provide direction and a sense of purpose, acting as a roadmap for your development journey. They should be specific, measurable, attainable, relevant, and time-bound (SMART). For instance, if you aim to improve your public speaking skills, a SMART goal might be to deliver a presentation at a local community event within three months. This goal is specific (public speaking), measurable (delivering a presentation), attainable (a local event), relevant (improving a valuable skill), and time-bound (within three months).

Once goals are set, creating a plan to achieve them is crucial. This plan should outline the steps needed to reach each goal, identify potential obstacles, and propose strategies to overcome them. For example, if your goal is to learn a new language, your plan might include enrolling in a language course, practicing daily with language apps, and joining a conversation group. By breaking down the goal into manageable steps, the process becomes less daunting and more actionable.

Self-awareness plays a significant role in continuous self-improvement. Understanding your strengths and weaknesses allows you to focus your efforts where they are most needed. Self-assessment tools, such as personality tests and skills inventories, can provide valuable insights. Additionally, seeking feedback from others can offer a different perspective on areas for improvement. Constructive criticism, when viewed as an opportunity for growth rather than a personal attack, can be incredibly beneficial.

Embracing a growth mindset is essential for continuous self-improvement. Coined by psychologist Carol Dweck, a growth mindset is the belief that abilities and intelligence can be developed through dedication and hard work. This mindset fosters a love for learning and resilience in the face of challenges. Instead of seeing failure as a setback, those with a growth mindset view it as a valuable learning experience. For instance, if you fail to secure a desired promotion, analyze what went wrong, seek feedback, and use the insights to improve your skills and performance for future opportunities.

Time management is another critical component of continuous self-improvement. Efficiently managing your time allows you to allocate sufficient resources to your development activities without neglecting other responsibilities. Techniques such as the Pomodoro Technique, where you work in focused intervals with short breaks in between, can enhance productivity and prevent burnout. Prioritizing tasks using methods like the Eisenhower Matrix, which categorizes tasks based on their urgency and importance, helps ensure that you focus on what truly matters.

Another powerful tool for self-improvement is mindfulness. Mindfulness practices, such as meditation and deep breathing exercises, help you stay present and reduce stress. Being mindful allows you to approach challenges with a clear and focused mind, making it easier to learn from experiences and make thoughtful decisions. For example, taking a few minutes each day to practice mindfulness can improve your concentration, emotional regulation, and overall well-being, all of which contribute to your ability to grow and develop.

Learning from others is an invaluable aspect of continuous self-improvement. This can be achieved through mentorship, networking, and observing role models. A mentor can provide guidance, support, and valuable insights based on their own experiences. Networking with peers and professionals in your field can expose you to new ideas, trends, and best practices. Observing and emulating the habits and behaviors of successful individuals can also offer practical strategies for improvement. For instance, if you admire a colleague's organizational skills, take note of their methods and try to incorporate similar practices into your routine.

Reading is another fundamental practice for continuous self-improvement. Books, articles, and research papers offer a wealth of knowledge on a vast array of topics. Whether you are looking to deepen your expertise in a specific field or broaden your understanding of new subjects, reading can provide the information and inspiration needed to fuel your growth. Make it a habit to read regularly, and choose materials that challenge your thinking and expand your horizons.

Taking courses and attending workshops or seminars are also effective ways to enhance your skills and knowledge. Many organizations offer professional development opportunities that can help you stay current with industry trends and advancements. Additionally, online platforms provide access to a wide range of courses on virtually any topic. Whether you are looking to improve your technical skills, learn a new hobby, or gain leadership training, there are resources available to support your goals.

Practicing self-care is crucial for maintaining the energy and motivation needed for continuous self-improvement. Physical health, mental well-being, and emotional balance all play a role in your ability to learn and grow. Ensure that you are getting adequate sleep, eating a balanced diet, exercising regularly, and taking time to relax and recharge. For example, incorporating regular physical activity into your routine can boost your energy levels, enhance your mood, and improve your cognitive function, all of which are essential for effective learning and development.

Reflection is a powerful practice that can enhance your self-improvement efforts. Regularly taking time to reflect on your experiences, progress, and setbacks allows you to gain insights and adjust your strategies as needed. Journaling is a practical way to capture your thoughts and reflections. By writing about your achievements, challenges, and lessons learned, you can monitor your growth over time and identify patterns that can inform your future actions.

Finally, resilience and perseverance are key to continuous self-improvement. The path to growth is often filled with obstacles and setbacks, and it is important to stay committed to your goals even when faced with difficulties. Developing resilience involves building the mental and emotional strength to bounce back from adversity and continue moving forward. For instance, if you encounter a major setback, such as a failed project or a personal challenge, focus on what you can learn from the experience and how you can use it to improve.

Chapter 4

Building Effective Communication Skills

The Power of Effective Communication

Effective communication is the lifeblood of any successful relationship, whether personal or professional. It goes beyond merely exchanging information; it's about understanding the emotions and intentions behind the information. Developing strong communication skills can lead to better relationships, increased productivity, and a more positive work environment.

Imagine a workplace where misunderstandings are minimal, feedback is constructive, and everyone feels heard and valued. This is the power of effective communication. It starts with active listening, which involves more than just hearing words. It requires fully concentrating, understanding, responding, and remembering what is being said. For instance, when a colleague is explaining a problem, an active listener will not interrupt but will instead nod, maintain eye contact, and provide feedback that shows they understand the issue at hand.

Non-verbal communication also plays a crucial role. Body language, facial expressions, posture, and eye contact can significantly impact how your message is received. Consider a manager delivering feedback with crossed arms and a stern face. The employee might perceive the feedback as negative, regardless of the words spoken. On the other hand, a manager who maintains open body language and a warm expression can convey the same feedback in a more positive and constructive manner. Being mindful of your non-verbal cues ensures that your message aligns with your intended emotions.

Clarity and conciseness are essential in avoiding misunderstandings. When communicating, especially in writing, aim to be clear and to the point. This means structuring your message logically and avoiding jargons or overly complex language that might confuse the reader. For example, when sending an email to a team about project updates, clearly outline the status, next steps, and any actions required from recipients. This reduces the chances of misinterpretation and ensures that everyone is on the same page.

Empathy is another powerful component of effective communication. It involves putting yourself in the other person's shoes to understand their feelings and perspectives. Empathy can transform a simple conversation into a meaningful connection. For instance, if a team member is struggling with a heavy workload, acknowledging their stress and offering support can make a significant difference. This not only fosters a supportive environment but also encourages open and honest communication.

Feedback, when given effectively, can be a tool for growth rather than a source of conflict. Constructive feedback should be specific, focused on behavior rather than personality, and delivered in a way that encourages improvement. For example, instead of saying, "You're always late," which can feel like a personal attack, try, "I've noticed you've been arriving after the start time. How can we adjust your schedule to help you get here on time?" This approach focuses on the behavior and offers a solution, making the feedback more constructive and less confrontational.

Conflict resolution is an inevitable part of communication, especially in diverse teams. Effective communication skills can help navigate conflicts smoothly and reach a resolution that satisfies all parties involved. When addressing a conflict, it's important to remain calm, listen to all perspectives, and work towards a solution collaboratively. For instance, in a scenario where two team members disagree on a project approach, facilitating a discussion where both parties can express their views and seek common ground can lead to a win-win situation.

Storytelling is a powerful way to communicate ideas and values. People are naturally drawn to stories, and they can make complex information more relatable and memorable. For instance, a leader sharing a personal story about overcoming a challenge can inspire and motivate their team. The story not only conveys the message but also builds a connection with the audience, making the communication more impactful.

Adapting your communication style to your audience is crucial. Different people have different communication preferences, and what works for one person might not work for another. For example, some people prefer detailed, written communication, while others might respond better to brief, verbal updates. Understanding these preferences and adapting your style accordingly can enhance the effectiveness of your communication. This is particularly important in diverse teams where cultural differences might influence communication styles.

Technology has revolutionized the way we communicate, offering various tools to enhance efficiency and reach. However, it's important to use these tools wisely. Emails, instant messaging, video conferencing, and social media each have their place, but knowing when and how to use them can make a big difference. For instance, while emails are great for detailed information, instant messaging might be better for quick updates or clarifications. Video conferencing can bridge the gap when face-to-face meetings aren't possible, adding a personal touch to the communication.

Building a culture of open communication within a team or organization can lead to increased trust, collaboration, and innovation. Encouraging team members to share ideas, ask questions, and provide feedback creates an environment where everyone feels valued and heard. Regular team meetings, open-door policies, and anonymous suggestion boxes are some ways to promote open communication. For instance, a company that holds regular town hall meetings where employees can voice their concerns and ideas is likely to have a more engaged and motivated workforce.

Listening to understand, not just to reply, is a fundamental aspect of effective communication. Often, people listen with the intent to respond rather than to truly understand the other person's perspective. This can lead to misunderstandings and missed opportunities for connection. Practicing active listening involves giving your full attention to the speaker, acknowledging their message, and responding thoughtfully. This not only shows respect but also ensures that the communication is meaningful and productive.

Effective communication is also about being authentic and transparent. Authenticity builds trust and credibility, making it easier to connect with others. Being transparent about your intentions, decisions, and even your mistakes can foster an environment of trust and openness. For instance, a leader who openly discusses the challenges the company is facing and the steps being taken to address them is likely to gain more trust and support from their team than one who hides the truth or communicates only selectively.

Developing effective communication skills is an ongoing process that requires practice and reflection. Seeking feedback from others on your communication style and being open to learning can help you continuously improve. Additionally, observing and learning from effective communicators can provide valuable insights and techniques that you can incorporate into your own practice.

Listening as a Leadership Skill

Listening is often underrated, yet it is one of the most powerful skills a leader can possess. It is more than just a passive activity; it involves actively engaging with and understanding the person speaking. When leaders listen effectively, they build trust, foster collaboration, and drive better outcomes.

Effective listening starts with being fully present. This means setting aside distractions and focusing entirely on the person speaking. Imagine a team meeting where the leader is constantly checking their phone. The team will likely feel undervalued and disengaged. In contrast, a leader who maintains eye contact, nods in understanding, and asks thoughtful questions demonstrates their commitment to the conversation. This presence not only shows respect but also encourages more open and honest communication.

Empathy is a critical component of listening. It involves putting oneself in another's shoes and understanding their feelings and perspectives. For example, consider a situation where an employee is struggling with a heavy workload. An empathetic leader listens to their concerns, acknowledges their stress, and offers support, whether through delegating tasks or providing resources. This approach not only addresses the immediate issue but also strengthens the relationship between the leader and the employee, fostering loyalty and motivation.

Listening also involves interpreting non-verbal cues. Body language, tone of voice, and facial expressions can provide significant insights into what is being communicated beyond words. A leader who can read these cues is better equipped to understand the underlying emotions and concerns of their team. For instance, if a team member says they are fine but their body language suggests otherwise, a perceptive leader might gently probe further to uncover any underlying issues.

Providing feedback is an integral part of listening. Constructive feedback helps individuals grow and improve, but it must be delivered effectively. Feedback should be specific, focused on behavior rather than personality, and given promptly. For example, instead of saying, "You need to be more organized," a leader could say, "I noticed the report was submitted late. Let's discuss how we can manage deadlines more effectively in the future." This approach is clear, actionable, and supportive, encouraging the individual to improve without feeling attacked.

Listening fosters a culture of inclusivity and collaboration. When team members feel heard and valued, they are more likely to contribute their ideas and engage actively in their work. A leader who regularly seeks input from their team and genuinely considers their opinions demonstrates that everyone's voice matters. This inclusivity can lead to more innovative solutions and a stronger sense of community within the team.

Conflict resolution is another area where listening proves invaluable. In any team, conflicts are inevitable, but how they are managed can make a significant difference. A leader who listens to all parties involved, acknowledges their perspectives, and works collaboratively towards a resolution can turn conflicts into opportunities for growth. For example, if two team members disagree on a project approach, a leader who listens to both sides and facilitates a constructive discussion can help them find common ground and move forward productively.

Listening also enhances decision-making. By gathering diverse perspectives and fully understanding the context of a situation, leaders can make more informed and effective decisions. For instance, before implementing a new process, a leader might seek input from various team members to understand potential challenges and benefits. This thorough approach ensures that decisions are well-rounded and considerate of different viewpoints, leading to better outcomes.

Building trust is essential for effective leadership, and listening is a key element in this process. When leaders consistently listen to their team, they demonstrate reliability and respect. Trust is built over time through consistent actions, and listening plays a significant role in this. For example, a leader who follows through on commitments made during conversations shows that they value their team's input and are dependable. This trust is fundamental to creating a strong, cohesive team.

Listening also plays a crucial role in personal development for leaders. By seeking feedback from their team and genuinely listening to it, leaders can identify areas for improvement and grow in their role. This humility and willingness to learn set an example for the entire team, fostering a culture of continuous improvement. For instance, a leader who regularly asks for feedback on their communication style and takes steps to improve based on that feedback demonstrates a commitment to personal and professional growth.

To effectively listen, leaders must also manage their own biases and assumptions. Everyone has preconceived notions that can influence how they interpret information. Acknowledging and setting aside these biases allows leaders to listen more

objectively and fairly. For example, if a leader
assumes that a quieter team member has less to
contribute, they might miss valuable insights. By
actively challenging this assumption and encouraging
input from all team members, the leader ensures a
more inclusive and comprehensive understanding of
the team's dynamics.

Listening is not always easy, especially in high-
pressure situations where quick decisions are needed.
However, even in these moments, taking a brief pause
to listen can lead to better outcomes. For instance, in
a crisis, a leader might feel the urge to act
immediately. However, by taking a moment to listen
to the team's input, the leader can gather crucial
information that informs a more effective response.
This balance between urgency and deliberation is a
hallmark of effective leadership.

In today's diverse and dynamic work environments,
communication styles can vary significantly. Effective
leaders recognize these differences and adapt their
listening strategies accordingly. For example, some
team members might prefer direct, straightforward
communication, while others might appreciate a more
nuanced, empathetic approach. By understanding and
respecting these preferences, leaders can ensure that
their listening is effective and supportive for everyone
involved.

Listening also extends beyond verbal communication.
Written communication, such as emails and reports,
requires careful attention to detail and context. A
leader who takes the time to read and understand
these communications thoroughly demonstrates
respect and consideration. For instance, responding

thoughtfully to an email rather than skimming and giving a quick reply shows that the leader values the sender's message and is engaged in the conversation.

Non-Verbal Communication

Much of what we communicate goes beyond words, conveyed through body language, facial expressions, gestures, and even silence. Non-verbal communication forms a substantial part of our interactions and can significantly influence how messages are received and interpreted. Understanding and mastering non-verbal cues can enhance one's effectiveness in both personal and professional relationships.

Consider a scenario in a business meeting. A manager presents a new strategy to the team. As she speaks, she notices one team member leaning back with crossed arms and a furrowed brow. This non-verbal cue suggests skepticism or discomfort, prompting the manager to address any concerns directly, thereby fostering open dialogue. Conversely, another team member sits forward, nodding and maintaining eye contact, indicating engagement and agreement. By recognizing these signals, the manager can tailor her approach to ensure the message is clearly understood and well-received.

Facial expressions are among the most potent forms of non-verbal communication. Human faces can convey a wide range of emotions, from happiness and surprise to anger and sadness. A simple smile can make a person appear friendly and approachable, while a frown can signal displeasure or confusion. For instance, during a negotiation, maintaining a neutral yet attentive facial expression can help in keeping the atmosphere professional and respectful, ensuring that both parties feel heard and understood.

Eye contact is another critical component. It can convey confidence, interest, and sincerity. However, the cultural context matters significantly. In some cultures, direct eye contact is seen as a sign of confidence and honesty, while in others, it might be perceived as rude or confrontational. Understanding these cultural nuances is essential for effective communication. For example, in Western cultures, maintaining eye contact during a conversation is generally expected and appreciated, suggesting that the speaker is engaged and trustworthy. In contrast, in some East Asian cultures, prolonged eye contact might be considered disrespectful, and a more subtle gaze is preferred.

Gestures, too, play a pivotal role. They can emphasize points, indicate direction, or even replace words entirely. A thumbs-up can signal approval, while a wave can mean hello or goodbye. However, gestures can also be easily misinterpreted if not used appropriately. Consider the "OK" hand sign: in some cultures, it signifies that everything is fine, but in others, it can be offensive. Thus, being aware of the cultural context and the specific meanings of gestures is crucial.

Posture and body orientation also communicate volumes. An open posture, with arms and legs uncrossed and facing the person you're speaking to, conveys openness and attentiveness. On the other hand, a closed posture, with crossed arms or legs, can suggest defensiveness or disinterest. For instance, in a job interview, sitting up straight and leaning slightly forward can demonstrate enthusiasm and eagerness, making a positive impression on the interviewer.

Touch is another powerful yet often overlooked aspect of non-verbal communication. A handshake, pat on the back, or even a gentle touch on the arm can convey warmth, reassurance, and connection. However, the appropriateness of touch varies widely across cultures and individuals. In a professional setting, a firm handshake can establish rapport and trust, but it's essential to gauge the other person's comfort level and cultural background to avoid any discomfort or misunderstanding.

Proxemics, or the use of personal space, also plays a significant role. Different cultures have varying norms for the appropriate distance between individuals during interactions. In some cultures, close proximity during conversation is normal and even expected, while in others, it might be seen as intrusive. For example, in Middle Eastern cultures, people might stand closer to each other during conversations compared to North American or Northern European cultures, where more personal space is typically maintained. Understanding these norms can help in navigating social interactions more effectively.

Silence, though often overlooked, is a powerful non-verbal tool. It can indicate thoughtfulness, agreement, or even discomfort. In some cultures, such as Japan, silence is valued and seen as a sign of respect and contemplation. In other contexts, prolonged silence might be uncomfortable and perceived as a lack of engagement. Knowing how to interpret and use silence can enhance communication and avoid misunderstandings. For example, during a brainstorming session, allowing moments of silence can give team members time to reflect and come up with more thoughtful contributions.

Appearance and attire also convey non-verbal messages. The way one dresses can influence perceptions of professionalism, competence, and respect. In a business setting, dressing appropriately for the occasion shows respect for the norms and expectations of the environment. For instance, wearing a suit to a formal business meeting signals seriousness and professionalism, while more casual attire might be suitable for a creative brainstorming session. Paying attention to grooming and attire helps in setting the right tone and making a positive impression.

Paralanguage, which includes tone, pitch, and volume of voice, adds another layer to non-verbal communication. The way something is said can be just as important as what is being said. A warm, enthusiastic tone can make a message more engaging, while a flat or monotonous tone might suggest disinterest. For example, delivering feedback in a calm and supportive tone can make it more constructive and less likely to be perceived as criticism.

Incorporating effective non-verbal communication requires self-awareness and practice. Being mindful of your own body language, facial expressions, and tone can help you convey your messages more clearly and effectively. Observing and interpreting the non-verbal cues of others can also provide valuable insights into their feelings and reactions. For instance, during a presentation, noticing audience members' body language can help you gauge their engagement and adjust your delivery accordingly.

Providing Constructive Feedback

Feedback is an essential tool for growth and development, whether in a professional setting or personal relationships. When delivered constructively, feedback can inspire improvement, foster learning, and build stronger connections. However, providing feedback effectively requires skill, empathy, and a strategic approach.

One of the first steps in providing constructive feedback is to ensure it is timely. Feedback given long after the event or behavior in question loses its impact and relevance. Imagine a scenario where an employee submits a project report with several errors. If the manager waits weeks to address the issue, the employee might not recall the specifics, and the opportunity for immediate learning is lost. Instead, addressing the issue soon after it occurs ensures that the feedback is relevant and actionable.

Specificity is another crucial element. Vague feedback can be confusing and unhelpful, leaving the recipient unsure of what actions to take. For example, telling someone, "You need to be more proactive," is less helpful than saying, "I noticed you missed the deadline for the client report. Proactively setting reminders for key deadlines could help manage your tasks better." The latter provides clear, actionable advice that the recipient can implement.

Balancing positive and negative feedback is also important. While it's essential to address areas needing improvement, recognizing and reinforcing positive behaviors can motivate and encourage the recipient. For instance, in a performance review, a manager might say, "Your presentation skills are excellent and have significantly improved our client engagements. However, I've noticed some delays in your project timelines. Let's discuss strategies to help you manage your time more effectively." This approach acknowledges the employee's strengths while also addressing areas for development.

The way feedback is framed can significantly impact how it is received. Using "I" statements rather than "you" statements can make the feedback feel less accusatory and more collaborative. For example, saying, "I noticed the report had several errors, and I think it would be beneficial to review it more thoroughly before submission," is more constructive than, "You made a lot of mistakes in the report." The former focuses on the issue and how to address it, while the latter can feel more like a personal attack.

Empathy plays a critical role in delivering feedback. Understanding the recipient's perspective and being mindful of their feelings can make the feedback process more effective and less confrontational. Consider a situation where an employee is underperforming due to personal issues. A manager who acknowledges this and offers support, rather than just criticism, is more likely to foster a positive outcome. For instance, saying, "I understand you've been facing some challenges outside of work. How can we support you to ensure these don't impact your performance?" shows empathy and a willingness to help.

Providing feedback in a private setting is also essential, especially when addressing sensitive or negative issues. Public criticism can be humiliating and damaging to the recipient's confidence and morale. Conversely, positive feedback can be given publicly to reinforce good behavior and set an example for others. For instance, praising an employee's excellent work in a team meeting can boost their confidence and motivate others to strive for similar recognition.

Active listening is a vital component of the feedback process. Encouraging the recipient to share their perspective and genuinely listening to their response can lead to a more productive dialogue. For example, after providing feedback on a project, a manager might ask, "How do you feel about the feedback? Do you have any suggestions on how we can address the issues together?" This approach fosters a two-way conversation and shows that the feedback is not just about pointing out flaws but about finding solutions collaboratively.

Focusing on behavior rather than personality is crucial in providing constructive feedback. Criticizing someone's character can be damaging and demotivating. Instead, addressing specific behaviors and their impact can lead to more positive outcomes. For instance, instead of saying, "You're not a team player," it's more constructive to say, "I noticed you've been working independently on projects that could benefit from team collaboration. How can we ensure you're more involved with the team moving forward?"

This focuses on the behavior and how it can be improved without attacking the individual's character.

Feedback should also be an ongoing process rather than a one-time event. Regular, consistent feedback helps individuals understand their progress and areas needing continuous improvement. This approach creates a culture of open communication and continuous learning. For example, implementing regular check-ins or performance reviews can provide opportunities for ongoing feedback and ensure that any issues are addressed promptly.

Providing actionable suggestions is another key aspect. Feedback should not only highlight what needs improvement but also offer concrete steps to achieve it. For instance, if an employee's writing skills need enhancement, suggesting specific training programs or offering to review their drafts can provide clear paths for improvement. This makes the feedback practical and achievable.

It's essential to recognize the effort and progress made by the recipient. Acknowledging incremental improvements can motivate continued effort and reinforce positive behavior. For example, if an employee has been working on improving their punctuality, a manager might say, "I've noticed you've been arriving on time more consistently. Keep up the good work." This recognition can boost morale and encourage the individual to maintain their efforts.

The tone and delivery of feedback also matter greatly. A calm, respectful, and supportive tone can make feedback more palatable and constructive. Conversely, a harsh or condescending tone can lead to defensiveness and resistance. Practicing empathy and maintaining a positive, solution-focused approach can significantly enhance the effectiveness of the feedback.

Finally, self-reflection and openness to feedback from others are crucial for anyone providing feedback. Understanding one's own biases and being open to constructive criticism can improve one's ability to give feedback effectively. For example, a manager might seek feedback from their team on their leadership style and how they can improve. This openness demonstrates a commitment to personal growth and sets a positive example for the team.

Communicating Vision and Goals

For any organization, clear communication of vision and goals is a cornerstone of success. A well-articulated vision provides direction, inspires employees, and aligns efforts towards a common purpose. Goals, on the other hand, break down this vision into actionable steps, ensuring that everyone knows what is expected and how to achieve it. Effectively communicating these elements can transform an organization, fostering a culture of clarity, motivation, and collective achievement.

Consider the story of a startup tech company, TechWave, aiming to revolutionize the way people interact with technology. The founders, Sarah and Alex, had a compelling vision: to create seamless, intuitive tech experiences that empower individuals and businesses alike. However, as their team grew, they realized that merely having a vision was not enough; they needed to communicate it effectively to ensure everyone was on the same page and equally passionate about the mission.

The first step they took was to craft a clear and concise vision statement. They distilled their broad aspirations into a single, powerful sentence: "Empowering everyday lives through intuitive technology." This statement became the North Star for TechWave, guiding their decisions and strategies. A vision statement should be aspirational yet attainable, providing a long-term direction that resonates with everyone in the organization.

Once the vision was clearly defined, the next challenge was to communicate it effectively to their team. Sarah and Alex organized a company-wide meeting where they shared the vision, explaining its origins and significance. They used storytelling to make it relatable, recounting personal anecdotes about their experiences with technology and their desire to make it more accessible and user-friendly. This approach helped to humanize the vision, making it more tangible and inspiring for their employees.

However, a vision alone is not sufficient without concrete goals to support it. Sarah and Alex understood that to achieve their vision, they needed to set specific, measurable, achievable, relevant, and time-bound (SMART) goals. They broke down their overarching vision into strategic objectives, such as developing user-friendly software, expanding their customer base, and fostering a culture of innovation within the company.

Communicating these goals required a structured approach. They held departmental meetings to discuss how each team could contribute to the overall objectives. For instance, the development team was tasked with creating new software features based on user feedback, while the marketing team focused on increasing brand awareness through targeted campaigns. By aligning individual and team goals with the company's vision, Sarah and Alex ensured that every employee understood their role in achieving the broader mission.

Regular updates and transparent communication were crucial in maintaining alignment and motivation. Sarah and Alex implemented weekly check-ins and quarterly reviews to track progress and address any challenges. During these sessions, they encouraged open dialogue, allowing employees to voice their ideas and concerns. This practice not only kept everyone informed but also fostered a sense of ownership and accountability.

Moreover, they recognized the importance of celebrating milestones and successes. Acknowledging achievements, both big and small, reinforced the connection between individual efforts and the company's vision. For example, when the development team successfully launched a new software feature, Sarah and Alex organized a celebratory event to recognize their hard work and dedication. These moments of recognition helped to sustain motivation and morale, reinforcing the belief that their collective efforts were driving the company towards its vision.

Visual aids and internal communication tools also played a significant role in keeping the vision and goals top of mind. TechWave utilized intranet platforms, digital dashboards, and visual progress trackers displayed in common areas to reinforce their objectives. These tools provided a constant reminder of the company's direction and allowed employees to see how their contributions were making an impact.

In addition to internal communication, Sarah and Alex understood the importance of external communication in reinforcing their vision. They actively shared their vision and progress with stakeholders, customers, and partners through newsletters, social media, and public speaking engagements. This transparency not only built trust but also created a sense of community and shared purpose beyond the confines of the company.

Challenges inevitably arose, and Sarah and Alex faced moments of doubt and resistance. There were times when market conditions changed, or internal dynamics shifted, requiring them to adapt their strategies. During such times, they revisited their vision and goals, reassessing and realigning them as necessary. Flexibility and resilience were key, ensuring that the vision remained relevant and achievable despite external pressures.

Sarah and Alex also invested in leadership development, understanding that effective communication of vision and goals extended beyond the founders. They nurtured a cadre of leaders within the organization who could champion the vision and inspire their teams. Regular training sessions and leadership workshops equipped these leaders with the skills to communicate effectively, manage change, and foster a positive organizational culture.

The impact of their efforts became evident over time. TechWave not only achieved its strategic goals but also cultivated a highly engaged and motivated workforce. Employees felt connected to the company's vision and understood how their roles contributed to its success. This sense of purpose translated into higher productivity, innovation, and employee retention.

Through their journey, Sarah and Alex learned several key lessons about communicating vision and goals:

1. **Clarity and Consistency**: A clear and concise vision statement that is consistently communicated can serve as a powerful guide for the organization.

2. **Engagement and Involvement**: Involving employees in the goal-setting process and encouraging open dialogue fosters a sense of ownership and commitment.

3. **Regular Updates and Transparency**: Keeping everyone informed about progress and challenges through regular updates builds trust and accountability.

4. **Recognition and Celebration**: Acknowledging achievements reinforces the connection between individual efforts and the company's vision, sustaining motivation and morale.

5. **Adaptability and Resilience**: Being flexible and willing to reassess and realign vision and goals in response to changing conditions ensures continued relevance and achievability.

6. **Leadership Development**: Investing in leadership development ensures that the vision and goals are effectively communicated and championed at all levels of the organization.

Chapter 5
Cultivating Emotional Intelligence

Understanding Emotional Intelligence

Emotional intelligence (EI) is a critical skill that influences how we manage behavior, navigate social complexities, and make personal decisions that achieve positive results. Unlike cognitive intelligence, which is static, emotional intelligence can be developed and enhanced over time. Understanding its components and learning how to harness them can significantly improve personal and professional relationships.

Emotional intelligence is typically broken down into five key components: self-awareness, self-regulation, motivation, empathy, and social skills. Each of these components plays a crucial role in how we interact with others and how we handle our own emotions.

Self-awareness is the foundation of emotional intelligence. It involves recognizing and understanding one's own emotions, strengths, weaknesses, values, and drivers. This self-knowledge is essential for managing one's responses to different situations. For example, consider a manager who is aware that they tend to become defensive when their ideas are challenged. By acknowledging this tendency, they can take proactive steps to remain open and

receptive to feedback, ultimately fostering a more
collaborative and innovative team environment.

Developing self-awareness requires introspection and
reflection. One effective method is to keep a journal,
noting down daily interactions, emotional responses,
and the triggers behind them. Over time, patterns will
emerge, providing insights into recurring emotional
reactions and the underlying causes. Additionally,
seeking feedback from trusted colleagues, friends, or
mentors can provide an external perspective,
highlighting blind spots and areas for improvement.

Self-regulation, the next component, builds on self-
awareness. It involves managing one's emotions in a
healthy and constructive manner. This does not mean
suppressing or ignoring emotions but rather
understanding and controlling them. For example, in
a high-pressure situation, a self-regulated individual
can stay calm and composed, making rational
decisions rather than impulsive ones driven by
anxiety or anger.

Techniques such as mindfulness and stress
management can enhance self-regulation.
Mindfulness practices, like meditation or deep-
breathing exercises, help individuals become more
aware of their emotional state and create a mental
space to respond thoughtfully rather than react
impulsively. Stress management strategies, such as
regular physical exercise, adequate sleep, and hobbies,
can also reduce emotional volatility, enabling more
consistent and balanced responses to challenges.

Motivation, another crucial aspect of emotional
intelligence, refers to the drive to achieve goals for

personal growth rather than external rewards like money or status. Intrinsic motivation is characterized by a passion for the work itself and the pursuit of learning and improvement. Individuals with high motivation are often more resilient, persistent, and committed, even in the face of setbacks.

Cultivating motivation involves setting clear, achievable goals that align with one's values and passions. Breaking down larger objectives into smaller, manageable tasks can make the process less overwhelming and more rewarding. Celebrating small wins and progress along the way can also sustain motivation and reinforce a positive mindset.

Empathy, the ability to understand and share the feelings of others, is a key component of emotional intelligence that enhances interpersonal relationships. Empathetic individuals can tune into the emotional signals of others, providing support and understanding. This skill is particularly valuable in leadership, customer service, and any role that involves teamwork and collaboration.

To develop empathy, practice active listening. This means fully concentrating, understanding, responding, and remembering what the other person is saying. Avoid interrupting or planning your response while the other person is speaking. Instead, focus on their words, tone, and body language. Reflecting back what you've heard and asking clarifying questions can also demonstrate empathy and build deeper connections.

Finally, social skills, which encompass a range of interpersonal abilities, are essential for effective communication and relationship management. These skills include communication, conflict resolution, teamwork, and influence. People with strong social skills can build rapport, manage conflicts, and collaborate effectively with others.

Improving social skills involves enhancing both verbal and non-verbal communication. Effective communicators are clear, concise, and considerate. They pay attention to their body language, facial expressions, and tone of voice, ensuring that their non-verbal cues align with their words. Additionally, developing conflict resolution skills, such as finding common ground and negotiating win-win solutions, can improve relationships and outcomes in both personal and professional settings.

Consider the story of Jane, a project manager at a multinational corporation. Jane was technically proficient and highly intelligent, but she struggled with team dynamics and leadership. Her projects often faced delays due to poor communication and unresolved conflicts. Recognizing the need for improvement, Jane embarked on a journey to enhance her emotional intelligence.

Jane started with self-awareness. She began journaling her interactions and emotions, identifying patterns and triggers. This practice revealed that she often felt frustrated when team members did not meet her expectations, leading to a perception of her being overly critical. Armed with this insight, she worked on self-regulation techniques, such as taking deep breaths and pausing before responding in stressful situations.

To boost her motivation, Jane set personal goals related to team development and project success, rather than just meeting deadlines. She celebrated small milestones with her team, fostering a sense of shared achievement. By aligning her goals with her values and passions, she found greater fulfillment and drive in her work.

Jane also focused on empathy, making a conscious effort to listen actively and understand her team members' perspectives. She practiced summarizing what she heard and asking questions to clarify their viewpoints. This approach not only improved her relationships with her team but also helped her to address their concerns more effectively.

Finally, Jane honed her social skills by attending workshops on communication and conflict resolution. She learned techniques for giving constructive feedback, managing difficult conversations, and building consensus. Her improved social skills led to better team cohesion, increased productivity, and a more positive work environment.

Over time, these efforts transformed Jane into a more effective and respected leader. Her projects ran more smoothly, her team was more engaged and collaborative, and she experienced greater job satisfaction. Jane's story illustrates the profound impact that developing emotional intelligence can have on personal and professional success.

The Four Components of Emotional Intelligence

Emotional intelligence (EI) is a multifaceted skill set that profoundly influences our personal and professional lives. It encompasses the ability to recognize, understand, manage, and utilize emotions effectively. By breaking down emotional intelligence into its four core components—self-awareness, self-regulation, social awareness, and relationship management—we can gain a clearer understanding of how to cultivate and apply EI in various contexts.

Self-awareness is the cornerstone of emotional intelligence. It involves recognizing and understanding our own emotions, as well as how they affect our thoughts and behaviors. This component requires a deep sense of introspection and honesty. For example, consider a scenario where you receive critical feedback from a colleague. If you are self-aware, you can identify your immediate emotional response—perhaps defensiveness or frustration—and understand why you feel that way. This awareness allows you to process the feedback constructively rather than reacting impulsively.

Developing self-awareness can be achieved through various practices. One effective method is keeping an emotion journal, where you document your feelings and the events that trigger them. Reflecting on these entries can reveal patterns and help you understand how your emotions influence your actions. Additionally, mindfulness meditation can enhance self-awareness by encouraging you to observe your thoughts and feelings without judgment.

Self-regulation builds upon self-awareness by enabling you to manage your emotions in healthy ways. It involves controlling impulsive reactions, maintaining composure under pressure, and behaving in ways that align with your values. Imagine a leader in a high-stress situation who must make quick decisions. A self-regulated leader can stay calm, think clearly, and act decisively without being overwhelmed by anxiety or anger.

To improve self-regulation, it's essential to develop coping strategies and stress management techniques. Deep-breathing exercises, regular physical activity, and adequate sleep can help maintain emotional balance. Moreover, cognitive reframing—challenging negative thought patterns and replacing them with more positive perspectives—can mitigate impulsive reactions and promote rational decision-making.

Social awareness, the third component of emotional intelligence, involves understanding and empathizing with the emotions of others. It requires tuning into verbal and non-verbal cues, such as tone of voice, facial expressions, and body language. Socially aware individuals can navigate social dynamics effectively, making them adept at building rapport and fostering positive relationships.

Empathy is a crucial aspect of social awareness. It allows you to put yourself in someone else's shoes and understand their perspective. For instance, if a team member seems unusually quiet during a meeting, a socially aware person might recognize signs of discomfort or stress and address the issue with sensitivity. Active listening is another key skill within social awareness. By giving full attention to the speaker, asking clarifying questions, and reflecting on what is said, you demonstrate respect and build trust.

Relationship management, the final component, involves using social awareness to build and maintain healthy relationships. It encompasses a range of skills, including effective communication, conflict resolution, and teamwork. Strong relationship management skills are essential for leaders, as they foster a collaborative and supportive work environment.

Effective communication is at the heart of relationship management. It involves not only expressing your thoughts and feelings clearly but also being receptive to the messages of others. For example, during a team meeting, a leader with strong relationship management skills will articulate their vision clearly, encourage input from team members, and address any concerns openly. This approach ensures that everyone feels heard and valued.

Conflict resolution is another critical aspect of relationship management. Conflicts are inevitable in any setting, but how they are handled can make a significant difference. A person skilled in relationship management will approach conflicts with a problem-solving mindset, seeking win-win solutions that satisfy all parties involved. This might involve mediating discussions, identifying common interests, and negotiating compromises.

Teamwork and collaboration are also essential elements of relationship management. Building a cohesive team requires understanding each member's strengths and weaknesses and facilitating an environment where everyone can contribute effectively. A leader with strong relationship management skills will delegate tasks appropriately, provide constructive feedback, and celebrate collective achievements.

Consider the story of Michael, a project manager at a software development company. Initially, Michael struggled with team dynamics and project deadlines. He often reacted impulsively to setbacks, causing friction within the team. Recognizing the need for change, Michael decided to develop his emotional intelligence.

Michael began with self-awareness. He kept a journal to track his emotional responses and identify triggers. Over time, he noticed that he became particularly stressed when projects fell behind schedule. Understanding this, he worked on self-regulation techniques, such as deep-breathing exercises and positive self-talk, to manage his stress more effectively.

Next, Michael focused on social awareness. He made a conscious effort to observe his team's body language and listen actively during meetings. This allowed him to identify when team members were feeling overwhelmed or disengaged. By showing empathy and addressing their concerns, Michael began to build stronger connections with his team.

To improve relationship management, Michael worked on his communication and conflict resolution skills. He practiced articulating his expectations clearly and encouraged open dialogue within the team. When conflicts arose, he approached them with a problem-solving attitude, seeking solutions that benefited everyone involved.

Michael's efforts paid off. His team became more cohesive, project timelines improved, and the overall work environment became more positive. By developing his emotional intelligence, Michael transformed his leadership style and significantly enhanced his team's performance.

Enhancing emotional intelligence is a continuous process that requires dedication and practice. It's not about suppressing emotions but understanding and managing them effectively. By cultivating self-awareness, self-regulation, social awareness, and relationship management, individuals can navigate the complexities of human interactions with greater ease and achieve more meaningful and productive relationships.

The benefits of emotional intelligence extend beyond the workplace. In personal relationships, EI fosters deeper connections, better communication, and increased empathy. It helps individuals manage stress, overcome challenges, and make more informed decisions. Ultimately, emotional intelligence contributes to overall well-being and success in various aspects of life.

Developing Empathy

Empathy, the ability to understand and share the feelings of others, is a cornerstone of emotional intelligence and an essential skill for building meaningful relationships. It goes beyond mere sympathy, as it requires us to put ourselves in someone else's shoes and truly grasp their emotional experience. Developing empathy can transform our interactions, enhance our communication, and foster deeper connections in both personal and professional settings.

Empathy begins with active listening, a skill that allows us to fully engage with and comprehend another person's perspective. Active listening involves more than just hearing words; it requires paying attention to non-verbal cues, such as body language, facial expressions, and tone of voice. For instance, imagine a colleague is explaining a challenging situation they faced at work. By maintaining eye contact, nodding in acknowledgment, and responding with thoughtful questions, you demonstrate that you are genuinely interested in their experience and willing to understand their emotions.

One effective way to practice active listening is to reflect on what the other person is saying. This technique, known as reflective listening, involves paraphrasing their words and emotions to show that you are engaged and empathetic. For example, if a friend expresses frustration about a difficult project, you might respond, "It sounds like you're feeling overwhelmed by the project's demands and the tight deadlines." This not only validates their feelings but also encourages them to share more, deepening your understanding of their perspective.

Empathy also requires us to be open-minded and non-judgmental. It's important to approach each interaction with a genuine curiosity about the other person's experiences and emotions, without jumping to conclusions or making assumptions. This mindset allows us to appreciate the complexity of their situation and respond with compassion. For instance, if a team member is consistently late to meetings, instead of immediately assuming they are irresponsible, consider asking about any challenges they might be facing that could be affecting their punctuality. This approach fosters a more supportive and empathetic work environment.

Another crucial aspect of empathy is emotional regulation. To empathize effectively, we must manage our own emotions and reactions. This means staying calm and composed, even when confronted with someone else's intense emotions. For example, if a family member is expressing anger or frustration, it's essential to avoid becoming defensive or reacting emotionally. Instead, take a deep breath, acknowledge their feelings, and respond with understanding. This not only helps de-escalate the situation but also demonstrates your ability to empathize and support them in a constructive manner.

Empathy can be further developed through perspective-taking, which involves imagining yourself in another person's situation and considering how you would feel and react. This practice can be particularly useful in resolving conflicts and fostering understanding. For instance, if a colleague disagrees with your approach to a project, try to see the situation from their point of view. Consider their concerns, values, and motivations, and use this insight to find common ground and work towards a mutually beneficial solution. Perspective-taking not only enhances empathy but also promotes collaboration and cooperation.

In addition to these interpersonal techniques, self-awareness plays a vital role in developing empathy. By understanding our own emotions, biases, and triggers, we can better manage our responses and connect with others on a deeper level. Regular self-reflection and mindfulness practices can help cultivate this self-awareness. For example, at the end of each day, take a few moments to reflect on your interactions and consider how your emotions influenced your responses. This practice can provide valuable insights into your empathetic abilities and areas for growth.

Consider the story of Sarah, a manager at a marketing firm. Sarah often found herself frustrated with her team's performance, leading to frequent conflicts and misunderstandings. Realizing the need for change, she decided to focus on developing her empathy skills. She began by practicing active listening, making a conscious effort to fully engage with her team members during meetings. She also adopted a non-judgmental approach, seeking to understand the challenges her team faced rather than jumping to conclusions. Over time, Sarah noticed a significant improvement in her relationships with her team. Conflicts decreased, communication improved, and the team became more cohesive and motivated.

Beyond the workplace, empathy can also enhance personal relationships. For instance, in a romantic relationship, empathy allows partners to understand and support each other's emotional needs, fostering a deeper connection and intimacy. Imagine a scenario where your partner is feeling stressed about work.

Instead of offering unsolicited advice or dismissing their feelings, practice active listening and reflective listening. Show that you understand their stress and are there to support them. This empathetic approach can strengthen your bond and create a more supportive and loving relationship.

Empathy also plays a crucial role in parenting. By empathizing with their children's emotions, parents can build trust and foster open communication. For example, if a child is upset about a conflict at school, instead of immediately offering solutions, parents can listen actively, validate their child's feelings, and help them process their emotions. This approach not only helps the child feel understood but also teaches them the importance of empathy and emotional intelligence.

Developing empathy requires continuous practice and a willingness to grow. It involves actively engaging with others, managing our own emotions, and seeking to understand different perspectives. While it can be challenging at times, the rewards are profound. Empathy enhances our relationships, improves communication, and fosters a more compassionate and connected world.

Managing Stress and Emotions

Life's unrelenting pace often brings about an array of stressors that can overwhelm even the most resilient among us. Whether these stressors stem from work, personal relationships, or unexpected challenges, managing stress and emotions effectively is crucial for maintaining both mental and physical well-being. The key lies in developing practical strategies that not only alleviate immediate stress but also build long-term emotional resilience.

At the heart of managing stress is the ability to recognize its presence and understand its sources. Stress manifests in various ways—physically, emotionally, and behaviorally. For instance, you might notice tension headaches, a short temper, or changes in sleep patterns. Identifying these signs early can help you address stress before it escalates. Take, for example, a professional who finds themselves increasingly irritable and fatigued. By acknowledging these symptoms as stress indicators, they can begin to explore and address the underlying causes, rather than simply treating the symptoms.

Mindfulness is a powerful tool for managing stress. By focusing on the present moment, mindfulness practices help reduce anxiety about the future and regrets about the past. One effective mindfulness technique is deep breathing. When you feel overwhelmed, take a few minutes to breathe slowly and deeply, inhaling through your nose and exhaling through your mouth. This simple practice can lower your heart rate and calm your mind, making it easier to approach stressful situations with clarity.

Another beneficial mindfulness practice is meditation. Regular meditation sessions can train your mind to remain calm and focused, even in the face of stress. Consider starting with just five minutes a day, gradually increasing the duration as you become more comfortable. For instance, a teacher dealing with the pressures of grading and classroom management might find solace in a daily meditation routine, helping them to reset and approach their responsibilities with renewed energy and perspective.

Beyond mindfulness, exercise is a well-documented stress reliever. Physical activity releases endorphins, the body's natural mood lifters. Whether it's a brisk walk, a yoga session, or a vigorous workout at the gym, exercise can help dissipate the physical tension that often accompanies stress. Imagine a busy executive who incorporates a morning run into their daily routine. This not only provides a healthy outlet for stress but also sets a positive tone for the day ahead.

Equally important is maintaining a healthy work-life balance. In today's connected world, the boundaries between work and personal life can easily blur, leading to chronic stress. Setting clear boundaries is essential. This might involve designating specific times for work and leisure, or creating a physical workspace separate from your living area. For instance, a remote worker might establish a rule to shut down their computer at 6 PM each day, ensuring they have time to unwind and engage in personal activities.

Time management skills also play a critical role in managing stress. Procrastination can exacerbate stress, leading to a last-minute rush that heightens anxiety. By prioritizing tasks and breaking them into manageable steps, you can reduce the pressure and create a more organized approach to your responsibilities. Consider the case of a student juggling multiple assignments. By creating a detailed schedule and adhering to it, they can tackle each task systematically, alleviating the stress of looming deadlines.

Social support is another vital component of stress management. Sharing your thoughts and feelings with trusted friends or family members can provide emotional relief and perspective. Sometimes, simply talking about your stressors can lighten the load. For example, a new parent struggling with the demands of childcare might find comfort and advice in conversations with more experienced parents, helping them to feel less isolated and more supported.

When stress becomes overwhelming, it's important to seek professional help. Therapists and counselors can offer valuable strategies and support for managing stress and emotions. Cognitive-behavioral therapy (CBT), for example, is an effective approach that helps individuals identify and change negative thought patterns that contribute to stress. Imagine an entrepreneur facing the pressures of running a startup. By working with a therapist, they can develop coping mechanisms and tools to handle the inevitable setbacks and challenges more effectively.

In addition to these strategies, fostering emotional resilience is crucial for long-term stress management. Emotional resilience involves the ability to bounce back from adversity and adapt to challenging situations. Building resilience often begins with self-compassion—treating yourself with the same kindness and understanding you would offer a friend. This means acknowledging your feelings without judgment and giving yourself permission to take breaks and seek support when needed.

Maintaining a positive outlook can also enhance emotional resilience. While it's natural to feel down during stressful times, focusing on positive aspects of your life can help shift your perspective. Gratitude practices, such as keeping a gratitude journal, can remind you of the good things in your life, providing a counterbalance to stress. For instance, someone going through a tough job transition might find solace in daily reflections on what they are thankful for, from supportive friends to personal achievements.

Developing problem-solving skills is another aspect of emotional resilience. When faced with a stressful situation, breaking it down into smaller, manageable parts can make it feel less daunting. This approach not only provides a sense of control but also helps generate actionable solutions. Consider a project manager dealing with a complex project. By identifying specific challenges and addressing them step by step, they can reduce the overall stress and create a clear path forward.

Lastly, humor and laughter are powerful antidotes to stress. Laughter triggers the release of endorphins, reduces stress hormones, and can even improve immune function. Finding moments of joy and humor in everyday life can provide a much-needed respite from stress. Imagine a healthcare worker navigating the pressures of their job. By sharing jokes and light-hearted moments with colleagues, they can build camaraderie and create a more positive work environment.

Applying Emotional Intelligence in Leadership

Leadership is more than just managing tasks and directing people; it's about inspiring and guiding a team towards a common goal. Central to effective leadership is emotional intelligence (EI), which involves recognizing, understanding, and managing one's own emotions while also being attuned to the emotions of others. Leaders who apply emotional intelligence can foster a positive work environment, enhance team performance, and navigate the complexities of interpersonal relationships with greater ease.

Consider a scenario where a team is facing a tight deadline on a critical project. The pressure is palpable, and tensions are running high. A leader with high emotional intelligence will first recognize their own stress and manage it effectively, setting a calm and composed example for the team. They might use techniques such as deep breathing or taking a brief walk to clear their mind before addressing the team. By maintaining their composure, they create a stable environment where team members can focus on their tasks without additional anxiety.

Understanding and managing one's own emotions is just the beginning. Leaders must also be adept at recognizing and empathizing with the emotions of their team members. Empathy is a cornerstone of emotional intelligence in leadership. When a team member is visibly stressed or upset, an emotionally intelligent leader will take the time to understand their perspective. This might involve a private conversation where the leader listens actively, validates the team member's feelings, and offers support. For example, if an employee is struggling due to personal issues, an empathetic leader might provide flexible work arrangements or direct them to available support resources.

Communication is another critical area where emotional intelligence plays a pivotal role. Leaders with high EI are skilled communicators who can convey their messages clearly and considerately. They understand that how something is said can be just as important as what is said. These leaders are mindful of their tone, body language, and the emotional impact of their words. For instance, when providing constructive feedback, an emotionally intelligent leader will choose their words carefully to ensure the feedback is perceived as helpful rather than critical. They might start by acknowledging the team member's efforts and then gently suggest areas for improvement, framing the conversation in a positive and supportive manner.

Building strong relationships within the team is essential for effective leadership, and emotional intelligence is key to this process. Trust and respect are fundamental components of any strong relationship, and leaders earn these by being consistent, reliable, and authentic. An emotionally intelligent leader is genuine in their interactions and transparent in their decision-making. They admit their mistakes and take responsibility for their actions, which fosters a culture of trust and accountability. For example, if a project doesn't go as planned, a leader might openly discuss what went wrong, what can be learned from the experience, and how the team can move forward together.

Another important aspect of applying emotional intelligence in leadership is conflict resolution. Conflicts are inevitable in any team, but how they are handled can significantly impact team dynamics. Leaders with high EI approach conflicts with a calm and open mindset. They seek to understand the underlying issues and the perspectives of all parties involved. Rather than assigning blame, they focus on finding mutually beneficial solutions. For instance, if two team members are in disagreement over a project direction, an emotionally intelligent leader might facilitate a discussion where each person can express their views and work together to find a compromise that aligns with the team's goals.

Emotional intelligence also involves fostering a positive team culture. Leaders can create an environment where team members feel valued, supported, and motivated. This includes recognizing and celebrating achievements, both big and small. An emotionally intelligent leader acknowledges the hard work and contributions of their team, which boosts morale and encourages continued effort. For example, a leader might regularly highlight individual and team successes in meetings or company communications, creating a culture of appreciation and recognition.

Self-awareness is a crucial element of emotional intelligence that leaders must cultivate. This involves being aware of one's own strengths and weaknesses and understanding how these can impact the team. A self-aware leader recognizes their own biases and works to mitigate them. They seek feedback from others and are open to personal growth and development. For example, a leader who knows they tend to be impatient might actively practice patience and mindfulness, ensuring they remain calm and supportive even in challenging situations.

Decision-making is another area where emotional intelligence is invaluable. Leaders often face complex decisions that require balancing various interests and emotions. Emotionally intelligent leaders consider the emotional impact of their decisions on the team and strive to make choices that are fair and empathetic. They involve the team in the decision-making process when appropriate, ensuring that everyone feels heard and valued. For example, when implementing a significant change, a leader might hold a team meeting to discuss the change, gather input, and address concerns, thereby fostering a sense of inclusion and collaboration.

Resilience is an important trait for leaders, and emotional intelligence contributes to building this resilience. Leaders with high EI can manage stress effectively and bounce back from setbacks. They model resilience for their team, demonstrating that challenges can be overcome with perseverance and a positive attitude. For instance, during a particularly challenging project phase, a resilient leader remains optimistic and focused, encouraging the team to keep pushing forward and find innovative solutions.

Lastly, emotional intelligence in leadership involves continuous learning and adaptability. The workplace is constantly evolving, and leaders must be able to adapt to new circumstances and challenges. Emotionally intelligent leaders are lifelong learners who seek out opportunities for personal and professional growth. They stay informed about industry trends, seek feedback from their team, and are willing to adjust their leadership style as needed. For example, a leader who notices a decline in team engagement might explore new motivational strategies or team-building activities to reenergize the team.